Rotherham Murders

Rotherham Murders

A half-century of serious crime 1900–1950

MARGARET DRINKALL

True Crime

First published in Great Britain in 2011 by
Wharncliffe Books
an imprint of
Pen and Sword Books Ltd
47 Church Street
Barnsley
South Yorkshire
S70 2AS

ISBN: 978-1-84563-138-3

A CIP catalogue record for this book is available from the British Library.

Typeset in 11/13pt Plantin by Concept, Huddersfield.

Printed and bound in England by CPI UK.

Pen & Sword Books Ltd incorporates the imprints of Pen & Sword Aviation, Pen & Sword Maritime, Pen & Sword Military, Wharncliffe Local History, Pen & Sword Select, Pen & Sword Military Classics, Leo Cooper, Remember When, Seaforth Publishing and Frontline Publishing.

For a complete list of Pen & Sword titles please contact
PEN & SWORD BOOKS LIMITED
47 Church Street
Barnsley
South Yorkshire
S70 2BR
England
E-mail: enquiries@pen-and-sword.co.uk
Website: www.pen-and-sword.co.uk

Contents

Introduction

Rotherham during the first half of the twentieth century was a town like any other in South Yorkshire. During those years its population had witnessed many events, including two world wars, industrial expansion, the eradication of slums and the laying down of plans for the housing estates we are familiar with today. Rotherham continues to progress and even today is going through a renaissance with the erection of modern buildings in the heart of the town. Little remains of the historic Rotherham of times past as we progress into the future and all that it holds, but hidden between the pages of newspapers are the stories of the crimes committed by persons who lived on the streets and roads that we are familiar with today. These heart-rending stories of crimes were real and indicate a society where two world wars had caused normal values to be broken down and death seemed somewhat closer than it had in

Soldiers parading down Doncastergate on their way to the training camps in 1914 (see Chapter 3). Rotherham Local Studies & Archives

previous years. These are the stories of some of the murders and attempted murders which took place in Rotherham in the first fifty years of the twentieth century.

Writing any book is team work and I would like to thank the staff at Pen and Sword Books and in particular Brian Elliott. I could not have written this book without the many nameless reporters of the *Rotherham Advertiser* who faithfully described the crimes at first hand for their waiting public. Sometimes the details were meant to shock and sensationalize and as a consequence errors were made; and in some cases I have had to use my own judgment and therefore any faults are mine. I would also like to acknowledge the staff at Rotherham Archives and Local Studies, without whose help I could not have completed this book.

I would also like to thank my son Chris Drinkall for his help with the photographs taken from the *Rotherham Advertiser* and the modern images of Rotherham as it is today.

CHAPTER 1

He Died Like an Englishman 1900

By 1900, the police force in Rotherham had become a more streamlined and professional group of men. Following the County and Borough Police Act of 1856, justices of the peace could now appoint rural police constables who would live and work in their own parish. Knowing the locality would ensure that such constables would know its inhabitants very well. The relationship between the population of these townships and their resident police constable worked generally quite well, although sometimes tensions would flare when police business had to be conducted. In July 1900, a constable doing his duty and delivering a summons taken out by another member of a family resulted in murder. Resentment had built up against the constable leading to his death and shocking both the community and his fellow colleagues.

On Saturday 14 July 1900, the population of the town of Rotherham read about a murder which had occurred in a little hamlet just outside Swinton called Piccadilly. The murder of a police constable always excites a community and this one was no exception. On Tuesday 10 July, PC John William Kew, a 29-year-old constable, heard a commotion coming from the back lane of a neighbouring house and, always the professional, went to see if he could help. He left at home his wife and four children. Kew was a constable with the West Riding Police

PC Kew. Rotherham Local Studies & Archives

Force stationed in Rotherham and had lived at the hamlet for the past five years. He was well thought of, respected in the neighbourhood and people would often turn to him to solve their problems rather than face the formal police station in the town centre. He had been born at Boston in Lincolnshire and for a short time had served with the Lincolnshire Constabulary, earning much credit for his ability and in the way he carried out his duties.

When Kew arrived at the scene of the argument at the back of a row of houses he found Charles Benjamin Backhouse, aged 23, with his wife and his younger brother Frederick Lawder Backhouse, aged 19. The family was known to be dysfunctional and a few weeks earlier Charles's wife had taken out a summons against her young brother-in-law, for assault. Frederick had not been in court and in his absence he had been fined 40s (£2) and costs. Henry Thompson, a neighbour to the Backhouse family, had warned Constable Kew that the two brothers had in their possession a revolver. This fact was probably uppermost in his mind when he arrived in the lane and saw the two brothers were arguing. He remonstrated with them both for causing a commotion and he told them that he was going to search them. At this point Charles stepped back, pulled out the gun and shot PC Kew, the bullet lodging in the upper part of his stomach. Despite his injury, this gallant police officer attempted to take the gun from Charles who casually handed the weapon to his younger brother Frederick who shot Kew once more, this time above his right hip. Unbelievably and despite his injuries, Kew managed to take Charles into custody and the two of them went back to the constable's house. When the constable's wife saw his injuries she called for a doctor who quickly arrived. Dr Fullerton sent for help to the local police station at Swinton and he made the injured man as comfortable as possible. Police Sergeant Danby arrived and handcuffed Charles, asking Kew in his presence what had happened. Kew indicated to say that Charlie had shot him and not to let him go. Charles, confronted by the two policemen, denied shooting Kew. When the sergeant left the house he saw Frederick outside the building, looking in through the window. Danby approached him and, after searching his person, found the gun in his trouser pocket. He arrested him and took him into the police house where once again in front of both brothers he asked Kew 'Who shot you?' Kew replied once again that Charles had shot him first, followed by Frederick. Charles said nothing whilst Frederick admitted that he shot Kew.

At this point there was no obvious reason for the shooting; witnesses stated that previously there had been no ill will shown to the policeman from the two brothers. But it later appeared that it had been Kew who had delivered the summons to Frederick from Charles's wife, but at the time neither man gave this as a reason. Kew's condition worsened and Dr Fullerton summoned the ambulance of the nearby Warren Vale Colliery. The stricken man was taken into Rotherham Hospital where he died at 2.00am, two hours after being shot. Both the arrested men were taken into custody and the next day they were visited by Charles's wife and their mother. It was reported that both women were very emotional and distressed. When the men were brought into court earlier that day the reporter noted that 'the men did not appear to understand the gravity of the charges made against them'. The magistrates remanded the brothers for seven days to allow further investigation into the matter.

It seems that on the day of the murder they had been drinking in a public house in Rotherham called the *High House*. There they met a neighbour from Piccadilly named Inkerman William Gibbons who was a bricklayer at Thrybergh Hall Colliery. Gibbons knew the brothers quite well and he told the court that they had entered the pub together about 9.30–10.00pm and left at closing time. He described the brothers as being a bit 'fresh', a euphemism for being drunk, and the three men walked back to Swinton together. On the journey Charles pulled out the revolver and showed it to Gibbons. He told him that it was a six-chambered weapon and it was primed and ready to use. His brother cautioned him, saying 'not tonight Charlie, in the morning'. Charles then put his fingers to his forehead and mimicked shooting himself in the head. Gibbons thought that Charles was contemplating suicide, but put it down to both brothers being intoxicated. Charles then stated that 'no man or women would alter what he had in mind' and when Gibbons asked him what was that he grandiosely said 'death or glory' and touched the pocket in which rested the gun. There strangely

High House, *the public house where the Backhouse brothers had been drinking shortly before the murder.* Chris Drinkall

also followed a conversation about where they were going to sleep that night. Gibbons was in lodgings with a family called Wheeler, but Frederick said that he was going to sleep out in the fields as he had done on previous occasions. Also, on the journey home, Charles stated mysteriously that 'they would not harm the mother or the children'. When Gibbons was asked about this in court he was asked to repeat this statement as it was crucial to the prosecutions case, indicating that the murder had been premeditated. The three men arrived in Swinton and went into the Wheeler household where Charles' wife, Annie Sanderson, along with Harriet Wheeler and her husband John were present. An argument ensued and Charles threatened Harriet saying, 'My God I will do for thee.' He was waving the gun around and Gibbons told him to put the gun away before it went off and killed somebody. The two brothers went outside with John Wheeler, followed by Mrs Wheeler and Annie Sanderson. The argument continued but when asked what it was about the brothers would not say, only stating that it was 'family business'. They were all congregated in the back lane, arguing, and this was where they were found by Kew. Gibbons said that only five minutes later he heard the first shot being fired.

The inquest on the body of Kew was held on 17 July 1900 at the West Riding Courthouse where large crowds had gathered. At the start both brothers were brought up from the police cells and it was noted by the reporter that Charles, although the oldest, was the shorter of the two brothers. Both men were dressed respectably and were wearing coloured neckerchiefs but both appeared to be unconcerned with the proceedings. The brother of the deceased, Harry Franklyn Kew, was first on the witness stand. He had identified the body of his brother in the mortuary and said that he had last seen him two years ago at Lincoln races. His brother had always been a healthy, kind and generous man who loved his job. He was well respected by his neighbours, was a happily married man and a good father to his four children. He told the jury that his brother had served with him at Boston in Lincolnshire, and though only serving for a short while, was extremely well thought of in the force. He described him as a young man in the prime of his life and his courage was evident in that he continued to carry out his duty even when he had been struck down by two bullets. The magistrate agreed that the deceased had acted with extreme bravery and condolences were offered to his wife and family. Kew was followed on the stand by the neighbour, Gibbons, then gave his statement to the jury. He said that when he heard the shot he had rushed outside and saw the group in the back lane. He heard Kew say to Charles, 'You have shot me Charlie what have you done that for? Have I done you any harm?' He stated that Charles was stood about a foot away from Kew. The gun was then passed from Charles to Frederick and he saw Frederick shoot at Kew one more time. A further witness, Henry Thompson, brother-in-law of the Backhouses, who lived at 14 Piccadilly, had also been at the *High House* in Rotherham on the night of the murder. He had been auditing the landlord's books. Thompson heard the two brothers discussing Kew and mentioning that Charles Backhouse had a revolver. On his return home he passed this information on to Kew and warned him about the brothers. Nevertheless, when the row started, Kew did not hesitate to do his duty. At this point in the proceedings, Mrs Backhouse senior, the mother of the two brothers, asked if she could speak. The coroner tried to dissuade her but she insisted. Crying piteously in between sentences, she complained that there had been no quarrelling prior to the shootings at the back of the Wheelers' house and that what had been discussed there was purely family business. She darkly hinted that there had been 'false swearing' given in evidence at the inquest before sitting down, her statement completed.

Dr James Sackville Martin, surgeon at the Rotherham Hospital, next took the oath. The *Rotherham Advertiser* noted that he took it in the 'Scottish fashion' with hand held up instead of being placed on the Bible. He stated that Kew had been brought into the hospital at 12.20am. He was perfectly conscious but had died at 2.02am. He had died from the penetration of two bullets although the bullets had not been found inside the deceased's body. He described the trajectory stating that the first bullet had gone into the large intestine causing the damage from which he had died. The coroner asked him if Kew would have lived if he had only received the second bullet, which had not hit any major organs rather than the first. Dr Martin agreed that it could have been possible to have saved him if only the last shot had been received. He described the blackening around the wound in the abdomen indicating that Kew had been shot at very close quarters. At this point the inquest was adjourned until the following Wednesday.

When the inquest was resumed the ironmonger who had sold the revolver to Charles Backhouse took the stand. He stated that his name was Thomas Brazier and he said that on the evening of the murder Charles Backhouse came into his shop on Broadway, Rawmarsh. He asked him if he had any guns for sale and on being showed two, he chose the one now exhibited as evidence in court which had cost 10s. Backhouse also bought nine cartridges. As he was leaving, Mr Brazier asked him if he wanted the gun to shoot cats and Charles said nothing, just smiled.

Next in the witness box was Sarah Ann Camm, wife of Herbert Camm, of Piccadilly, who had also witnessed the constable being shot twice, first by Charles and then by Frederick.

Harriet Wheeler and Annie Sanderson were next summoned into the court but curiously it appeared that both had been stricken with illness. The coroner asked the clerk if they had submitted doctor's notes which were then produced.

The coroner in his summing up advised the jury to find the prisoners guilty of wilful murder. He explained that to be guilty of murder a jury had to show that there was a common purpose to kill someone and that there was no doubt that both men had been involved in the act which had a common purpose to shoot PC Kew. After the arrest Frederick had admitted that they had done the murder but claimed that they were both drunk at the time, but the coroner told the jury to forget this statement as evidence showed that the murder had been pre-planned and therefore with 'malice aforethought'. He also told them that it didn't matter who had shot the fatal bullet and that both men were equally guilty in the eyes of the law. The jury did as they were directed and the accused were formerly committed for trial at the Leeds Assizes.

Kew's funeral was held on Saturday 21 July and was attended by a large crowd of people. Fifty members of the West Riding Constabulary were in attendance and the cortege was headed by Mrs Kew, her four children and Kew's brother. Such was the condemnation of this brutal act felt by the population of Rotherham that following the funeral a subscription was started for Mrs Kew, headed by a £5 donation made by the local MP, W H Holland. For several weeks the *Rotherham Advertiser* made the appeal for subscriptions for the family of PC Kew and listed the contributions.

Ten days later, the two prisoners were brought to trial at the West Riding Assizes held at the Town Hall in Leeds. It was reported that at the beginning of the trial the prisoners were as impassive as ever, until Charles' wife, upon giving evidence, broke down and cried. It was at this point that Charles put his head into his hands and seemed for the first time to recognise the enormity of his crime.

The barrister for the defence put up a good fight for the men's lives. He admitted that although Frederick had not tried to stop his brother or take the gun away from him, he had not fired the first shot. That had unquestionably been made by Charles and more significantly it was the shot which killed Kew. He suggested that reasonably all that Frederick could be charged with was aiding and abetting his brother to commit murder. The barrister stated that previous to the attack Charles had shown no ill will towards Kew and that the murder had been committed whilst he was temporarily insane through drink.

The jury took just one and a half hours to deliberate and came back into the court to deliver their verdict. Charles Backhouse was found guilty of the charge and his brother Frederick was charged with aiding and abetting. The judge asked the foreman of the jury, 'Do you find Frederick was a party to the murder before and at the time the murder was committed?' The foreman agreed that was correct. The judge pointed out that in that case the verdict amounts to guilty for both men. The foreman stated that the jury had asked for clemency for Frederick due to his young age and being influenced by his older brother. But the judge was having none of it as he donned the black cap and gave the death sentence to both of them. He said to the brothers 'that they should be taken from this place and hence to a place where they would be hanged from the neck until they were dead'. Only at this point did the prisoners appear to have taken in the seriousness of the crime of which they had committed and they both appeared to be very dazed at the outcome.

The *Rotherham Advertiser* of 18 August 1900 announced the execution of Charles Benjamin Backhouse, which had taken place at Armley Gaol. Despite the judge's decision, Frederick, in view of the recommendation of mercy from the jury, had been reprieved. It was reported that Charles Backhouse was to be part of a double hanging carried out that same day by executioner Billington. James Billington came from a family of executioners and on his retirement his sons took his place. The other prisoner hanged at the same time as Charles was a Leeds man called Tom Mellor, aged 32, who had murdered his two illegitimate children by drowning them. It was reported that large crowds gathered in front of the prison in order to see the black flag raised and was duly noted at 9.00am precisely. It was reported that Charles Backhouse had acted nobly and was perfectly resigned to his fate. He heard the news that his brother had been reprieved 'with great joy'.

The sacrifice of the life of PC Kew had been noted in the press and the patriotism of the time of the South African War ensured that the highest praise would be given to this man who it was reported had 'died like an Englishman'.

CHAPTER 2

'I Have Gone Mad' 1914

By July 1914 the town of Rotherham was preparing for war. On 10 August 1914 the Territorial Army, camped in Whitby over the bank holiday, were recalled and mobilized a few days later. The town turned out to wave them off as they marched down Doncastergate to the railway station and to war. But the fear of war and the privations which went with it possibly preyed on the minds of mothers to the extent where they felt that to end the life of themselves and their children would be better than having to endure years of warfare.

Sometimes when people are able to hide their state of mind, it is more of a shock for the partners. In this next case a father finished his shift at the pit and returned home to find the bodies of his wife and three of his children waiting for him. The case happened at Green Lane, Rawmarsh, when Emily Liversedge killed three of her four children and attempted to take her own life. The couple, both aged 37, had lived in the area for twelve years and were well known in the neighbourhood. Their neighbours stated that she was a hard working mother who appeared to be very fond of her family and he was a steady man, sober and industrious, having a regular job at Silverwood Colliery. A neighbour told a reporter from the *Rotherham Advertiser* that the couple always looked 'comfortable with each other and had both been brought up in Rawmarsh and had plenty of friends and relations in the area'. She also told him that Emily had been in service to Dr Naylor prior to her marriage.

The tragedy began after miner Arthur Liversedge completing a night shift. He reached home just after 7.30 on the morning of Thursday 16 July 1914 and, instead of being met by his wife as was her usual practice, was greeted by his 12-year-old son, Edgar, who let him into the house. Noticing that his son appeared frightened, he asked him what was wrong. Edgar told him that his mother had impressed on him to make sure that as soon as his father entered the house he had to read the note she had left for him on the kitchen table. Edgar watched his father, who upon reading the note, threw it on the kitchen floor and ran up the stairs to the two bedrooms. In the smaller bedroom he found the bodies of his four children laid out on the bed. Emmy (aged 6) and Jessie (3) were on top of the covers, and at their feet was the body of Doris (10), all of them with their throats cut and covered in blood, apart from Doris who was still alive. All the children were in their night clothes. Arthur shouted to Edgar to fetch Auntie Belinda who lived four doors away and then, realizing that he did not want her to see the children in this state, ran after his son and told him to fetch Uncle George instead. Returning back to the house, he saw the body of his youngest child, Belinda (6 months old), which had been washed, laid out, covered with a cloth and carefully placed on a table under the window of the bedroom. She also had a deep gash to her throat and there was a bloody razor on the floor by the children's bed. Going into the bedroom he shared with his wife he found her fully dressed on the floor, lying on her right side, with her throat cut. Another razor was found by her side. He noted that she also was still breathing. By now Uncle George, also known as 'Mr Parker', arrived. Seeing what had happened, George rushed to find a doctor and then to alert the police to the tragic events.

Police Constable Holmes from Rawmarsh station arrived first and he read the letter from Mrs Liversedge. This is what this poor, demented women had written to her husband:

> Dear Arthur,
> Keep and bless Edgar dearly as you love us all. Send for Mary Ann and her mother and my mother, Aunt Belinda and Mrs. Platt. Love for Horace and Emily and yourself. I have gone mad.

By now two doctors, Jago and Naylor of Rawmarsh, had arrived. Upon inspecting the bodies they attended to little Doris to try to keep her alive and attempted to staunch the wound from Emily. Despite her terrible injuries Doris was still able to speak, saying, 'Mamma did it'. Emily murmured pathetically,

'I love all my children. I wish I could die'. The two doctors quickly dispatched the bodies of little Doris and her mother to Rotherham Hospital, with the, by now distraught father, accompanying little Doris in the ambulance.

Inspector Somerset arrived at the house and he asked the doctors if they could pinpoint the time of death. They stated that it was approximately five or six hours earlier. The constable noted that Emily had either been up early or had not gone to bed at all as she was still fully dressed. Carefully planning what she was going to do, she lit a fire in the kitchen downstairs before going back upstairs to wake her son, Edgar. The latter told Inspector Somerset that he slept in the same bedroom as the girls and had gone to bed the previous night about 11.30pm. Prior to which, no doubt as a final treat, all the children had gone with their mother to the pictures in Rotherham. Just as Edgar was about to fall asleep Jessie had cried, wanting to get into bed with her mother. Emily picked her up out of the children's bed and carried her through into her own bedroom. He told the inspector that the following morning whilst it was still very early his mother had woken him, saying, 'Get up love and go downstairs and unlock the door for your father and pull the blind up. The fire is laid so let your dad in when he comes and don't forget to tell him to look for the note.' She bundled the poor young man out of the bedroom before he could see the bed containing the younger children. When asked by the coroner at the inquest whether he had noticed anything wrong in the bedroom Edgar admitted that he had been 'half awake and half asleep'. He had tried to go back to the bedroom, but his mother had firmly pushed him towards the stairs. He went down the stairs and lifted the blind and played with his cigarette cards in the kitchen until his father arrived home.

The inquest was held at the Council Offices, Rawmarsh Hill, the following day, 17 July, and the reporter described the scene. The case had attracted a lot of attention and consequently the crowds outside the offices were very large. The eyes of the crowd were turned to see Mr Liversedge arrive with his son Edgar at the stroke of twelve o'clock. Emily was still in hospital and her condition was described as serious. The coroner gave his condolences to Mr Liversedge and asked him if there had been any sign of distress or anything unusual in his wife's behaviour leading up to the murder. Mr Liversedge stated categorically that his wife's behaviour had been perfectly normal when he left for work and he had no idea what must have driven her to commit such a crime. The couple had no money worries and they had not had a quarrel; and had always been on good terms with each other. He stated that he had left his wife and family the previous evening at 8.30pm and had not noticed anything strange in the conduct of his wife. He did admit that she had always been passionately fond of the children to the point of obsession but nevertheless he was wholly unable to account for her actions. Some neighbours were called to give evidence and although they had seen Emily coming and going from the house during that last day there was nothing untoward in her behaviour. However, they did admit that she was sometimes noted as being 'quite excitable'. Another neighbour spoke to her about 5.00pm on the Thursday evening and she noticed nothing in her demeanor that caused her to think that anything was wrong. No sounds were heard coming from the house that evening and nothing appeared to be wrong until the grim discovery by Mr Liversedge when he returned from work.

Dr Naylor and Dr Jago gave evidence that the bodies had all had their throats cut with a razor which had been found at the scene. Dr Naylor gave his opinion that the wounds looked like they had been inflicted with some force, indicating the terrible action of a woman out of control. When questioned by the coroner, Dr Jago told him that the children would not have suffered and had died almost immediately from loss of blood. The bodies appeared to be well nourished, cared for and healthy; and the cause of death in all cases was injury to the throat. The coroner, Mr J Kenyon Parker, told the court that the condition of Mrs Liversedge and Doris was still a matter of grave concern and the jury could do no more for the time being. The inquest was to be adjourned for three weeks. If in the meantime Mrs Liversedge or Doris passed away he told the jury they would be called back. However, for that day it was enough to confirm identification of the bodies and to hear the medical evidence.

The funeral of the three children was held on Sunday 19 July at the Haugh Lane Cemetery. Six pictures in the local newspaper show crowds of people pressing closer to see the three

Crowds waiting in Green Lane for the funeral of the three children. Rotherham Local Studies & Archives

little coffins and the flowers that had been placed on the grave. On 5 August the inquest was resumed and once again the crowds outside the council offices were huge. Just before 2.00pm two taxis drew up and people pressed forward to see Emily emerge, accompanied by a woman attendant and a police officer. She looked pale and distraught. The second taxi held Mr Liversedge and Doris who refused to leave her father's side. Mr Liversedge refused to look at his wife. Emily, several times during the inquest, particularly when Edgar was giving evidence, started to weep, howl and shake her head. It was reported that during one of these piteous episodes that Doris said to her mother, 'Don't cry mamma, don't cry.' The coroner at this point felt that it would be better for Doris not to be in the

Mourners entering the funeral coaches. Rotherham Local Studies & Archives

The bodies of the three children on the way to the cemetery, Sunday 19 July 1914. Rotherham Local Studies & Archives

court room as the evidence was too upsetting and she was led out. As she passed, her mother held out her arms as if to sweep the child into her breast, but the child was led away. When the doctor related the injuries on the children Emily could not hold back her tears and wept copiously.

The coroner in summing up informed the jury that he did not intend to call Doris to the stand unless the jury insisted. But the members of the jury shook their heads. No one would wish to put the little girl through any more anguish than she had already suffered. He told them:

> The only question we have to consider today is who inflicted the wounds on the children and not to worry about

At the cemetery gates waiting for the funeral coaches to arrive. Rotherham Local Studies & Archives

Lowering the coffins into the grave. Note the small coffin carried by the funeral director under his arm and father behind marked with an 'X'. Rotherham Local Studies & Archives

the state of mind of the mother at the time of the murder. That will be decided by professionals.

The jury solemnly announced that Mrs Liversedge '. . . had wilfully murdered all three children, in the early hours of July 16th 1914'. The coroner asked for three separate verdicts of wilful murder for Emmy, Jessie and Belinda, which the jury complied with. When the verdict was given Emily fainted as the coroner sent her to be tried at Leeds Assizes. In the meantime she was to be kept at Armley Gaol in Leeds where the state of her mental health would be assessed. It was reported that when the couple left the offices that the crowds had reached 'enormous dimensions' and the 'greatest of sympathy' to

The grave where all the children were interred together and some of the floral tributes. Rotherham Local Studies & Archives

Mr Liversedge and Doris was expressed by some people in the crowd.

Emily appeared at the assizes in Leeds on 28 November 1914. She was still very distraught and was unable to speak in her own defence. Mr Liversedge gave his evidence in a firm clear voice, but his manner faltered when he spoke about finding the bodies. He once more told the court that he had no idea why she had killed the children. A Dr Walker was invited into the court and he spoke about assessing Emily as to her mental state. He told them that she was on medication to help her sleep. When asked by the coroner, the doctor gave his opinion that she was not in her right mind when committing the murders as she truly believed that her children would be better off dead, but could offer no reason as to why she should come to this decision. The judge summed up the case for the jury, saying that there was no reason given by Emily for committing the crimes; but it was the opinion of the doctors who specialized in such things that her reasoning was not what it should be. The jury took an hour to find Emily 'guilty but insane'. She quietly sobbed all through the hearing of the evidence and the verdict; and was still crying when they led her away.

The reason why Emily committed the murders was never established. But at the time she lived through a period of great stress and anxiety, not only for her but for the rest of the people of Rotherham. By July 1914 it was becoming clear that Great Britain would shortly be at war with Germany, officially declared the following month. To a fragile mind, the talk of forthcoming food privations, men having to be sent to fight in France, leaving their children behind; and the very real threat of invasion might have been sufficient to have tipped her mind over the edge. Perhaps by sending her children out of the world she truly believed that she was doing her best for them. No one had a bad word to say about Emily and the way she looked after her children. One can truly hope that in the mental institution she was sent to that she found the peace of mind she deserved.

CHAPTER 3

Attempted Murder at Hoober Stand

1916

In May 1916, it was a usual sight to see soldiers in the streets of Rotherham. It was even reported in the *Rotherham Advertiser* that 'khaki-mad young women were guilty of throwing themselves at anyone in uniform'. Now in the second year of the war, it was a common sight to see recruitment campaigns, displays and marching throughout the main streets. Looking at the newspapers of the period we see patriotic comments urging the men to enlist and fight 'the Hun'. Reports of 'German atrocities' filled the town. Not all the soldiers who paraded in khaki were the patriotic young men who were seen going off in their thousands from the station at Rotherham surrounded by loving families who never saw them again. Some of the men who enlisted were from the seedier parts of the town and not the fine upstanding characters loved by the propagandists.

This crime was brought to the attention of the Rotherham public when a newspaper of 12 June 1915 reported a cowardly attack on 'an old man', on the previous Sunday, 6 June. The victim was Arthur Crossley, the caretaker at the Hoober Stand, near to the village of Wentworth, just outside the town. Hoober Stand is a folly on the Wentworth Woodhouse estate of the Earl Fitzwilliam, a local landmark approximately 98 feet high and 600 feet above sea level, therefore visible for miles around. The stand was built in 1747/8 by Thomas Watson Wentworth who fought on the side of the King George II to celebrate the defeat of Jacobite rebels in 1745. For his efforts Wentworth was elevated to be a Marquis and his heirs became Earl Fitzwilliam. The monument and the nearby village of Wentworth attract thousands of tourists to the folly today and the site is noted to be a place where ghosts are frequently seen and felt by visitors

Hoober Stand, where Arthur Crossley was employed as caretaker. Rotherham Local Studies & Archives

to the area. One sighting shows a picture of a figure at the window of the building late at night. Is this the victim of the following case and is he still haunting the place where a soldier attempted to kill him?

In 1916, the military authorities had requested billets for soldiers in and around the Rotherham. These newly-enlisted men were being trained in Sheffield and needed accommodation for short periods. Arthur Crossley was one of the persons who opened his home to soldiers and two men were dispatched to his house. They were Private Archibald Evans, aged 22, and another unnamed soldier who was billeted with him from 11–19 May. The soldiers had been stationed at Redmires Camp, Sheffield and were undergoing training before being sent out to the Front. Crossley, who was reported to be a 'kindly old man', had lent them a revolver, cartridges and a flash lamp during their stay, which they returned to him when they left to go back to camp. They were expecting to get shipped out to France so it was with some surprise when Evans returned back to Crossley's house on 25 May and asked if he could stay another week. Crossley agreed. Evans stayed the night of the 25/26 May and on the following morning left the house at 10.00am, saying that he was going back to the camp. However, on his return at 5.30pm, he told Crossley that he had not been back to the camp and instead had been to Dunford Bridge and Elsecar. At 7.00pm Crossley said that if Evans was staying for the week he would need to buy some bread. Evans volunteered to go and get some bread for himself and his landlord but he never returned back to the house. Crossley, meantime, found that not only had Evans taken the revolver, cartridges and flash lamp, but had also helped himself to a lady's gold watch and long gold chain which had been kept on the dressing table in his bedroom. The gold

Soldiers in training camp. Rotherham Local Studies & Archives

watch and chain had belonged to his deceased wife and therefore had some special meaning to him. Understandably, he was angry that his hospitality had been so badly betrayed. Crossley reported the matter to the local police and they made enquiries at the camp but they told him that the chances of getting the stolen items back again was very slim. It was more than likely they would be pawned as quickly as possible. Given the evidence, Crossley doubted that he would see Evans again. The police were not wrong, and they were soon contacted by George Cotton the manager for Messrs Tyler Brothers, pawnbrokers, of Pond Street, Sheffield, who told the police that Evans had offered them a lady's gold watch and chain on 1 June. Cotton had questioned Evans to find out if it was his property and he replied that it was but he wanted to dispose of it. Evans told him that it was a watch he had bought for his girlfriend, but since then they had fallen out and he just wanted to have some money to get back to camp.

To Crossley's surprise, once again Evans turned up at his door at 8.30am on Sunday, 6 June, asking his former landlord how 'he was getting on'. Crossley queried his concern, saying,

'You were so unkind the last time that you were here.' He then challenged Evans to stealing the articles and the latter asked him if he had actually seen him taking them; and of course Crossley had to admit that he hadn't actually witnessed Evans doing this. In little towns and villages of those days doors were often left unlocked and Evans implied that anyone could have entered the house and stolen the items. Crossley saw his opportunity to have Evans captured and he asked him to come with him to have a look at some chalk marks which had been made on the Hoober Stand. His intention was to imprison Evans within the building, until he was able to call the police and have him taken into custody. The two men went out of the house, walking approximately 60–80 yards down the path when Evans told Crossley that he had left his stick at the back door. Crossley stated that Evans had not brought a stick with him, but due to the other man's insistence they went back to the house where, surprisingly, there was no stick.

By now Crossley had enough of his former lodger and he asked Evans to leave, walking down the path in front of him and opening the gate to let him out. As he stepped in front of him to open the gate Evans shot him in the back. After the first shot Crossley turned round to face Evans, putting up his hands as a sign that he was not going to struggle with the younger man. To his horror, Evans shot him again, asking 'Am I mad?' Crossley, knowing that Evans was intent on killing him, now began to struggle with his assailant. During the fracas Evans shot Crossley four more times, although none of the bullets penetrated him fatally. Crossley was now on the ground and Evans put the stolen revolver to Crossley's head and pulled the trigger. No doubt expecting to die, Crossley would have closed his eyes in anticipation of his certain death, but to his relief the gun just clicked, indicating that the barrel was empty. Evans knew the game was up and fled into a wood described as being 'near to Mr Hardy's farm'. Crossley, although still in a state of shock, managed to get to a neighbour's house and called the police. He was examined by Dr Mills, a local physician from Wentworth, who sent him into Rotherham Hospital where he took out the bullets the following day.

The police were now looking at an attempted murderer and Evan's description was sent out to other police stations and the camp at Redmires, with instructions that he should not be approached and was known to carry a gun, therefore to be considered dangerous. The wanted soldier was described as being aged 35 and 5 feet 5¾ inches tall, of a slim build, clean-shaven and a native of Penrith, Cumbria.

Evans was finally found at what was described as the 'chief pleasure ground at Sheffield', Endcliffe Woods. This recreational area was very popular and at the time was reported to be full of people. On Monday 7 June, two of his comrades from the camp had recognized him and, knowing that he had been involved in the attempted murder of the old man the previous night, kept him talking. Private William Harry Crookes and Private Lesley John Armitage were both stationed with the E Company of Sheffield City (Service) Battalion at Redmires Camp and were passing Endcliffe Woods about 9.00pm that evening when they spotted Evans. One of the men engaged him in conversation whilst the other summoned the police. Evans was arrested by Detective Officer Cope who took him to Castle Green police station and arrested him on the charge of the attempted murder of Arthur Crossley on the morning of Sunday 6 June. Evans was brought to the West Riding Courthouse at Rotherham on the following day and charged not only with the attempted murder but also of stealing the gold watch and chain, a six chambered revolver, and an electric flashlight, to the total value of £10. Dr Mills from the Rotherham Hospital told the court that Crossley was recovering well but although his injuries were very severe they were not dangerous nor life threatening. Evans, appearing in the dock in civilian clothing, denied all the charges, stating that 'he did not remember the incident'. Nevertheless he was found guilty and sentenced to be tried at the next Leeds Assizes.

Evans appeared at the Assizes on 16 July 1916 and was once again found guilty and sentenced to three years' imprisonment. The jury asked for clemency due to his young age but the judge pointed out that he was fortunate not to be on a higher charge as his actions indicated that when he went to Crossley's house that morning he had every intention of killing him. Thankfully, the feisty old pensioner was able to fight back and to save his own life, although he had no doubt that if the gun had gone off when Evans held it to his head he would have been instantly killed.

This case indicates very strongly that people intent on murdering another, for what ever reason, will usually stop at nothing to achieve those ends. Thankfully in this instance, Evans was thwarted in his desires and his victim lived. But does his ghost still haunt the Stand? To make your own mind up visit the website of www.rotherham-ghosts.com and you can judge for yourself.

CHAPTER 4

Murder of a Neighbour 1915

Only after the Second World War did the medical authorities really recognize that 'shell shock' affected the mind and unbalanced people and they started to look at the effects of this, and depression, on human behavior. Psychiatry was in its infancy and the working of the brain was a relatively unknown area to many medical people during the first few years of the century. Today, we have criminal profilers who would delve into the mind of such a murderer and see events which might trigger off the reasons for the murder. But in many cases even the murderer himself cannot explain. This case was so random and bizarre that it left the neighbourhood with more questions than answers.

On the morning of Thursday, 9 September 1915, Lucy Ann Martin, aged 39, went out into her backyard at North View, Swallownest, to hang out some washing, only pausing to have a short conversation with a young girl whose uncle lived next door. During the war years young people were encouraged to befriend and write to soldiers on the front line and they spoke briefly about a letter the young girl, named Edith Lynes, had received from such a pen pal. Lucy appeared to Edith to be her usual bright and cheerful self as they chatted. It was almost 1.00pm and as Edith turned away she noted that Lucy had a garment and two clothes pegs in her hand. As Edith went into the house she heard a loud bang and saw a car go past. Mistakenly, she thought that someone in the car had fired a gun. Then she saw the body of Lucy on the floor, with the garment and pegs still in her hand.

Another neighbour, Florence Oldfield, was sat at the back door of her house enjoying the sun. She also witnessed her neighbour falling to the floor as well as hearing the shot and seeing the car go by. Seeing the body on the floor shook her and,

Swallownest, where Lucy Ann Martin lived with her husband and seven children.
Rotherham Local Studies & Archives

thinking Lucy must have fainted, she rushed to her side only to see that top of her head was bloody. Lucy Martin was carried into the house and placed on the sofa, but it was apparent that she was already dead. Dr Fairbrother of Beighton was called and attended the house as quickly as possible. There, he declared her life extinct and questioned Mrs Oldfield as to what she had seen. Florence told him about the car that she and Edith had witnessed and described the army officer who had been driving the vehicle. It later turned out that this car and driver were traced and soon eliminated from the official enquiries. The doctor noted that the entrance wound was at the top of her head, indicating that the shot had been fired from above. The doctor called in the police.

Police Inspector Whincop and Sergeant Robinson were the first to arrive at the scene and they were soon joined by PC Shaw. A discussion took place with the doctor about what had happened and he pointed out the entrance and exit holes of the shot in the dead woman's skull. He asked Mrs Oldfield if Lucy had spoken at all before she died, but the poor woman had no time to utter a sound. They went out into the garden and asked Mrs Oldfield about the neighbour in the middle of hers and Lucy's house and were told that a man named John Johnson lived there. The man was aged 51 and had been something of a recluse. He rarely went out, lived alone and was known to be 'peculiar in his manner'.

Robinson and Shaw knocked on Johnson's door but the door was locked and there was no reply. Whilst the body was being removed the police held a house-to-house enquiry, but nothing more could be learned. Many neighbours admitted to hearing a shot, but, combined with the passing motorist, assumed that it had been the car backfiring. No one had a bad word to say about the deceased woman who it seems had been very hard working and respectable and a good mother to her seven children, the youngest one being only a few months old. An hour later, when there was still no sign of Johnson, it was decided that the two police officers, would attempt to enter his house through a ladder up to the bedroom window at the back. Shaw went up the ladder which was held by Robinson and shouted to his colleague that he could see a body. Robinson then went up the ladder and he also saw the body of a man in the corner of the bedroom. Johnson, the reclusive neighbour, was dead, having cut his throat with a razor. The gun which had shot Lucy was lying on the bed and was described as an old muzzle-loading gun which showed signs of having been recently discharged. The bedroom window from where he had shot the unfortunate victim had been deliberately held open by a tin tray placed on the windowsill. It was apparent from the body, which was cold, that the man had been dead for some time. The rest of the house was searched, but apart from being very chaotic, gave no evidence as to why he had decided to shoot his neighbour, a woman known to be a happy, contented person, who was extremely friendly and cheerful. There was no motive to the crime and the neighbours told the police officers that they had never heard a cross word between Lucy and Johnson.

The inquest on both bodies was held in the Baptist Chapel, Swallownest, on Saturday morning, 11 September 1915, before the district coroner, Mr Kenyon Parker. It had been decided that the inquest on the body of Mrs Lucy Ann Martin would be held first. The stories about the murder had excited the population of the town and there was reported to be a large crowd outside the chapel watching the coming and goings of the participants. The first witness was the husband, George Martin, who was a bank foreman at Beighton Colliery. He told the coroner and the jury that he had left his wife on the morning of 9 September to go to work at 5.40am. He described her as being in good health and spirits when he left her. Shortly after his lunch he was told about the death of his wife and that he had arrived home about 1.40pm, finding her body on the sofa. At first he was told that she had been shot at from a car, but later the doctor confirmed that she had been shot from above and the likelihood was that Mr Johnson had shot her; but both versions seemed to him to be implausible. At this point the coroner instructed the jury to ignore the details about the car as the matter had been investigated and the police were satisfied that the gun had not been fired from any vehicle, but had been fired from the neighbour's house. Martin expressed his puzzlement over the reason for the neighbour to shoot his wife. She had never complained about him and as far as he was aware Mr Johnson had no grievance against his wife. He told the court that they had little to do with Johnson who was some what of a recluse and seemed reluctant to talk, but he had always been very civil to the couple when spoken to. Dr Fairbrother, who attended the house, stated that on the right side of the deceased woman's face were eleven gunshot wounds and in his opinion they were consistent with being shot with a gun fired from above. During the post mortem he had noted that her internal organs were all in good condition and he attributed the cause of death to the shot penetrating the brain. Mrs Oldfield took the stand and corroborated her previous statement to the police that she saw Lucy fall but had no reason to give as to why Johnson should commit such a random act. The coroner summed up and he told the jury that they had heard all the evidence and it was therefore their task to decide whether the case was one of accident or intentional murder. The jury was so sure of the verdict that they chose not to retire from the room and it was unanimously agreed that wilful murder against John Johnson was recorded.

The coroner then agreed to hold the inquest on the body of Johnson and the first witness was his brother. He gave his name as Thomas Johnson of Main Street, Swallownest, and he told the coroner that he had last seen his brother about three weeks previously. He admitted that his brother lived a very solitary life and did not have any friends but even he couldn't offer any explanation as to why he would shoot his neighbour. He also stated that as far as he was aware there had been no dispute between the two neighbours. His brother had lived on his own for about three years and the condition of his mind had deteriorated during that time. He was very depressed. The coroner asked him if his brother had ever discussed suicide with him and Mr Johnson said he had not discussed it with him but he was aware that he had attempted suicide some years previously by the same method of cutting his throat with a razor. He did tell the coroner and the jury that another brother had died in an asylum and offered that 'he must have been out of his head' to have committed such a motiveless crime.

Dr Fairbrother then gave medical evidence to the inquest. He said that when he examined the body of John Johnson he found a deep gash on the left side of the neck which had been self inflicted. Johnson had been a patient of his and he had known the man for about twenty years. During that time he described him as having 'a dull, morose disposition due to the solitariness of his lifestyle'. Johnson would often not respond when spoken to and in his opinion the man had likely become insane and was not in his right mind when he committed the murder. The doctor offered the opinion that he would go so far as to categorize him as a homicidal maniac. He also stated that with their being no evidence as to the reason why he had chosen to kill Mrs Martin, he felt that there was a high probability that he would have killed anyone else who happened to be there at the time. The jury took no time at all in recording their verdict that Mr Johnson had committed suicide whilst of an unsound mind. The foreman of the jury, Mr Lomas, expressed sympathy to the family of Mrs Martin and the children and the coroner also added his consolation to the bereaved husband.

Lone gunmen attacking random people is more common today than it was in the early years of the twentieth century and psychologists still do not have a solution as to why certain people will decide to kill strangers. Was Johnson jealous of the happy family who lived next door from his solitary state? One thing is for sure that his random act must have devastated the family and set the whole of Swallownest talking about their version of the reasons for the killing for many years to come.

CHAPTER 5

Murder at Maltby 1918

Very much like today, young people were unable to afford their own homes just after the First World War when a national housing shortage was reported. It was far from the government's vision of 'houses fit for the returning heroes'. The workers in the Maltby Colliery were in a reserved occupation and the colliers of the township were busy maintaining outputs throughout the years of the war. Housing shortages meant that adult couples were forced to live with elderly parents and the strains on these kinds of relationship must have been evident. On Millindale in Maltby, one house at the end of the war was described as a 'two rooms upstairs and two rooms downstairs cottage' which was shared by a couple who had five children and who lived in the same two-bedroomed house as the father-in-law and the brother-in-law.

On the 28 September 1918 Maltby was rocked when the bodies of Alfred Ridgeway (aged 50), a collier, and his wife Elizabeth (45), had been discovered in the early hours of the morning. Alfred Ridgeway had been suffering from depression and paranoia for a few years. When Sergeant Blacker arrived on the scene he was told that a few days previously Ridgeway had quarreled with his wife and had moved out of the family home. The sergeant had been called to the scene by the father of the murdered woman, George Phillips, at 7.30am. He found the body of Alfred Ridgeway on the floor of the kitchen surrounded by blood. Next to him was a razor which he described as being 'wet with blood'. Sergeant Blacker noted that the main artery on the right hand side of Ridgeway's neck had been slashed. The body was cold and from this he deduced that the body had been dead for some time. The man was fully dressed apart from his coat which lay on a chair. Going upstairs, he found the body of Ridgeway's wife, Elizabeth, lying in the bed that she shared

Maltby Colliery where Alfred Ridgeway worked. Rotherham Local Studies & Archives

with the younger children and her throat was cut in a deep wound from the right side. Also in the bedroom was the bed shared by the older children. When the body of Elizabeth had been lifted, a razor was found hidden in the bedclothes. The police noted that a broken pane of glass near the back door was the way in which the intruder had got into the property. George Phillips told them that nothing had been stolen from the house and he suspected that the intruder was no one else but Ridgeway and that he had crept into his wife's bedroom where she was in bed and had cut her throat whilst the children slept beside her. He had then gone downstairs and had cut his own throat in the kitchen. The bodies were removed and an older sister was called upon to take care of the children. Phillips was then taken to Rotherham police station for further questioning and he was asked to give an explanation for his theory. He then told them an incredible tale.

Philips had been woken during the early hours of 28 September by George, one of his young grandsons, who said to him, 'My daddy is murdering my mummy.' He told the police that upon hearing the boy he got out of bed to look for the candle and matches which were usually kept by the side of the bed only to find that they were missing. He described the house as being pitch black and he could see nothing as he went downstairs. He pulled on his boots and went into the street where he shouted, 'Murder!' at the top of his voice.

What happened next defies belief. Unable to wake the neighbours or to get any assistance at all, he promptly went back to bed and back to sleep, not waking till daylight, when he noted it was 7.00am. In his statement he said that he had not seen or felt the body of his son-in-law when he was downstairs and even more unbelievably neither did he go into his daughter's bedroom to investigate the information from his grandson. There is no mention of whether Mr Phillips had been drinking the night before, but this is the only credible reason that I can imagine for this oversight. When he finally went downstairs in the morning light he found the body of Ridgeway and shouted upstairs to

Steel Peach & Tozer where Thomas Philips, where the brother of the murder victim worked. Rotherham Local Studies & Archives

his daughter, to come down and see, but of course there was no reply.

An inquest was called the following day at the police station in Maltby and the first on the stand was George Phillips. He told the coroner that he shared the house with Ridgeway and his daughter and their five children with his son Thomas Phillips. The coroner, Mr Kenyon Parker, was incredulous that there were nine people, four adults and five children sharing the one house where there were only two bedrooms. It seems the back bedroom was shared by the couple and had a single and double bed in it. The two youngest children shared the bed with their parents and the single bed was shared by the two older children who previously had shared with an older sister called Martha, now living elsewhere. The second bedroom was shared by himself and his son Thomas.

Martha gave evidence and told the court that her sister Bertha turned to her for help when she was asked to come to the house and 'settle things on Friday 27 September 1918'. Bertha told her that 'dad was kicking up a row and she thought he had gone mad'. He had accused his wife of having a relationship with her own brother and Martha of having incestuous relations with her uncle, Thomas Phillips. Martha went to the house to find her mother and father arguing. Ridgeway was adamant in his belief that both his wife and daughter were having a relationship with Thomas. Martha was appalled that her father could believe such lies and she denied it completely. She told him that she was not speaking to him again until he apologized, and left the house, never to see her father alive again.

Ridgeway seemed to get more and more upset and he told his wife that he could no longer stay in the house. He went upstairs and packed a box of his clothes and belongings and went to live in lodgings with another collier in Farquar Road, Maltby. The police had interviewed some of his workmates who told them that they had seen him on the Friday night and he had spoken to them about the argument with his wife, stating that he was jealous of his brother-in-law, but without repeating the allegations of the supposed intimacy. The same friends stated that, apart from expressing his feelings about his brother-in-law, he appeared to be 'his normal self'.

On Saturday 28 September Martha was woken once again by her sister who asked her to come to the house as their mother and father were dead. The horrified girl went to the house and saw the body of her father lying in the kitchen surrounded by blood. She then went upstairs to remove the two youngest children from the bed where she found the body of her mother under the bedclothes. The coroner asked about the state of her mother's body, but she told him that she did not investigate the body too much as she was intent on making sure that the two youngest children did not see their mother. However, she did note that there was blood on her mother's face, but that much of it had been covered by the bedclothes. She took the two children out of the room and back to her own house. The coroner asked her what her relations had been with her father prior to the accusation. She told him that her father had suffered for a long time from insomnia and had recently also complained of pains in his head. She also told the coroner that previously they had got on well but relations had become difficult between herself and her father since the false allegations which had been made by him and she had not spoken him since.

Bertha Ridgeway (10), next gave evidence. She said that on the Friday night her mother went up to bed, taking the two younger children, Gertrude (9) and the baby, with her. Bertha was in the single bed next to her mother's which she shared with George (8). Awaking at some point during the night she saw her father, who had not been in the house earlier, getting off the bed where her mother and the two children lay. He went downstairs and shortly afterwards she fell asleep again. She heard her mother groan which woke her up again and then she heard her say, 'This is my last.' She thought she heard her father call out 'murder' but wasn't entirely sure that she had heard correctly. As children do, she went back to sleep and told the coroner that she felt that it was a long time before she woke up again. Little George was asked what he remembered about the night of the murder. He said that he also saw his father sitting on his mother's bed and heard her mother saying, 'This is my last' and giving a groan. After his father had gone out of the bedroom, George went into his grandfather's bedroom and told him what he had seen.

Sergeant Blacker gave his evidence, stating that when he found the woman the body was still warm, but whether this was due to the bedclothes or from the bodies of the two younger children, who had only been removed minutes before, it was impossible to state. Going downstairs again, he noted that the kitchen window had been pushed open and he offered his opinion that this was where Ridgeway had made his entrance during the night. Scuff marks in the dust indicated where he had knelt whilst climbing into the house. The coroner asked if there was any indication that the murders had taken place the other way round and that Elizabeth had murdered him and then committed suicide. But the sergeant felt that, given the evidence, there was no possibility of the murder being undertaken in that fashion. The coroner then summed up the case and, addressing the jury, said:

> . . . that the allegations made by Ridgeway to his wife and daughter were not part of the case and they should not be gone into with any depth. No one could be sure about the truth of the matter and that they needed to concentrate on Alfred Ridgeway's motive on that evening. Did he deliberately go to the house with the intention of murdering his wife and doing away with himself? There was no evidence as to his state of mind at the time. On the contrary the friends he had spoken to had stated that he did not appear to be in a state of insanity.

The jury found that Alfred Ridgeway had 'murdered his wife and then committed suicide'. The funeral of the couple took place the following day. Large crowds turned out to watch and speculation about the reasons for the two deaths continued in Maltby long after the two bodies were buried.

It certainly seems that Ridgeway was under the misapprehension that his wife and daughter were having an affair with Thomas Phillips despite the fact that there appears to be little evidence to support this. Nevertheless, it does seem that this delusional fantasy fuelled the desire to murder Elizabeth and to take his own life. It is my belief that he was not in a balanced state of mind when he undertook the murder and suicide, but there was still a level of planning in order to gain entrance to the house and commit the deed. The actions of George Phillips are less easy to explain away and, as stated, can only mean that the man was intoxicated at the time. In every murder there are always innocent victims and in this case they were the children of the Ridgeways who lost their mother and father in a single night.

CHAPTER 6

Death of Annie Fellows 1919

This case also caused a sensation at Maltby. In November 1919, a 20-month-old child was so badly neglected by her father and stepmother that she died of starvation. Annie Fellows was born to Charles Edward Fellows and his wife Agatha in April 1918. They had a house on Hayhurst Crescent, Maltby, where the couple lived with their four other children aged from 11 years to the baby. He was earning £4–£5 a week and the couple seemed to be getting along quite well for a while. Trouble in the marriage started in May 1918, a month after Annie's birth, when Fellows (39), invited Emma Ratcliffe (42), to lodge with himself and his wife. Very soon afterwards it was evident to Mrs Fellows that he was sleeping with the lodger but knowing it would make no difference she kept silent. At first the arrangement appeared to work well but inevitably jealousy crept in, and on 31 August 1918 he ordered her and the children to leave the house. She had no option but to go to her mother's in Hucknell, Nottinghamshire, where she found a small house for herself and the four children. Matters deteriorated however and she was forced to enter the workhouse at Basford. All inmates to the workhouse had to prove what was called 'settlement' which was the need to prove to which area they were settled, in this case Rotherham. The guardians at Rotherham workhouse had to pay the expenses of the family and inevitably they ordered that they be removed back to Rotherham. Meanwhile, they summoned Fellows for maintenance for his wife and children. Rather than pay, he went to the workhouse at Basford and removed the three older children. However, Ratcliffe was not happy about this and in less than a fortnight the children were returned to the company of their mother and baby sister.

The family returned to the workhouse at Rotherham and later Mrs Fellows was offered a job in Nottingham. Knowing that it would be impossible to work and look after the children, she took them to Maltby on 11 October 1919, to live with their father. At this time all the children were healthy and well nourished. Annie was described by her mother as being a 'bonny baby who was never poorly'. She walked with the children for part of the way and then sent them alone for the final few yards to their father's house. When they knocked on the door they were greeted by Ratcliffe who did not seem pleased to see them saying, 'You are not b**** well going to stop here.' Their father was at work and when he returned home he asked the children who had sent them to him and the eldest child, Charles (11), told them that his mother had sent them. Fellows later said that he was pleased to see the children but there was not much evidence to prove this. All the children were forced to sleep on the floor of the kitchen in whatever bedding was available. He spoke to Police Sergeant Blacker of his predicament, no doubt under pressure from Ratcliffe, but the sergeant advised him to keep the children with him. Now that his wife was working she told him that she did not want any money from him towards maintenance, which must have relieved the situation to a certain extent. The children then appeared to have led a nightmare life with a father and stepmother who did not want them in the house. The hardest affected was on the baby of the family, perhaps because she was the last one born to Mrs Fellows. Ratcliffe resented her for that very fact.

Neighbour Agnes Pridgeon of Queen Street, Maltby had known Fellows for some time. On the Wednesday before the baby died she saw the three older children in the lane, but not Annie. On Thursday, she called at the house and saw the little girl sat near to the fireguard warming herself. She looked pale and wan and Pridgeon suggested as much to Ratcliffe saying, 'If she is not much better soon you will have to get a doctor to her.' Ratcliffe replied, 'I will if she gets no better.' Pridgeon saw her again the following day and she did not look much better and once again urged Ratcliffe to get a doctor to look at the child. Another neighbour, Arthur Chadwick, who lived two doors away from Fellow's house, saw the child on the same day when she appeared at his doorstep. This kindly man thought the little girl had a cold and he lifted her onto his knee for about twenty minutes or so. He finally gave the little girl a penny and she went home. It is my guess that this was the only friendly cuddle that little girl had in the last week of her life. On Saturday 18 October Fellows came to Pridgeon's house and said, 'Will you have a look at my Annie? I think she is about done.' Pridgeon went to the house on Hayhurst Crescent and suggested once more that a doctor be called. Ratcliffe was in the bedroom whilst this conversation took place and stayed in the bedroom when the doctor arrived. Dr Dufty arrived very shortly afterwards, but the little girl was already dead. Pridgeon tried to suggest that she had died of appendicitis, but Dr Dufty told her that he would do a post mortem on the body to find the cause of death. Dufty completed this on 20 October and found the vessels of the brain were congested, but otherwise there was no sign of disease in the little girl's body, nor was there any sign of food or water in the stomach. He related his concerns to Sergeant Hayes who went to see the couple, the latter asking them how they accounted for the fact that the baby had died of starvation. Fellows told him, 'Oh no sir, the baby had tinned milk in her tea.' The pair were brought before the coroner for the inquest on Tuesday 21 October.

The first witness was the child's mother who gave evidence against the couple. She was challenged by her husband as to the reason why he took the children away for almost a fortnight, but before she could answer the coroner told him that he was:

> in a serious position firstly by living with another woman and secondly the deceased was left at your house in a healthy condition and later died of starvation from which offence the jury would possibly send you for trial for murder or manslaughter. I am obliged to allow you to ask questions as you do not have a solicitor but I doubt that you are doing yourself any good.

Mrs Fellows stated that when she lived at the marital home with her husband she had milk delivered to the door by a milkman, Harry Wadsworth, who also corroborated the statement. He stated that he had delivered a half-pint of milk, a tiny amount considering the needs of a family of two adults and four children, but confirmed that since Mrs Fellows had left that he was not asked to deliver milk at the house. He also added that he knew of no other milkman who delivered milk to the family and that if he had been asked he would have been delighted to have continued the supply. Mrs Fellows told the coroner that she had in September gained a separation order against her husband which ordered him to pay 30s a week. However, it was not long until he reneged on the deal and she was forced to have him taken into custody. He was given a prison sentence for default of payment and as a result of this she was forced to take the children to her mother's house in Nottingham; and thence into the Basford Workhouse on 2 June where she remained until 9 October 1919 when she had been removed to Rotherham workhouse. She had been offered a situation and so she decided to take the children to their father's house.

Contradictory evidence was given by a lodger at the house at Hayhurst Crescent, Nellie Fishwick, a married woman living apart from her husband. Nellie had first gone to lodge at the house three weeks previously where Fellows and Ratcliffe, and Ratcliffe's daughter Adelaide lived. She remembered the day in which the four children came to the house and she had therefore seen a good deal of the little girl who she described as 'fretting for her mother'. She told the coroner and the jury that she had seen the child being fed three times a day including the two days before her death, when she claimed the child had two hot meals. On the very day of her death she had given her some tea, without milk, as Ratcliffe did not take any. Later she had given her some 'sops', which consisted of tea and bread, but the child had vomited this meal up again, and she later fed her a little bit of water. Nellie was unaware that anything was wrong with the child and was unaware of her death until she got up on the Saturday morning. She stated that Ratcliffe had looked after the child to the best of her ability, but significantly commented that the child appeared to 'want loving'. She stated that she had never seen the child ill-treated. This evidence was completely demolished by Dr Dufty who told the court of his finding no sign of water or food of any kind in the stomach of the child. He had undertaken another post mortem on the 23rd and had found absolutely no evidence to change his original cause of death.

But the most chilling evidence was given by the eldest son, Charles, who at that time was living back at the Rotherham workhouse. He told the coroner of Ratcliffe's less than friendly greeting when the children arrived at the house and stated that in the week before his little sister died he had never seen her fed. When questioned by a juror he said that he was at school every day, but at the time that he was in the house no food had been given to the child. On one occasion the little girl was crying for water and he asked Ratcliffe for permission to get her some, but she denied him. He told the coroner that the older children had food of sorts which mainly consisted of bread and lard three times a day, but that Annie was not given any food at all. During these meal times she wept and asked for 'cake' which was refused. On the Friday, the day before she died, he witnessed Ratcliffe hitting the child with the back with her hand.

Fellows denied his son's evidence, saying that he welcomed the children to his house warmly and that Ratcliffe had treated them properly, although she was admittedly annoyed that the children had been sent to her in such cold weather. He told the inquest that since the children's arrival he had got up every morning at 8.00am to get the children breakfast before he went to work and he had on occasions given Annie some dinner. He was followed into the witness stand by Mrs Ratcliffe who gave her version of events. She told the coroner that the little girl cried bitterly and she had done her best with her but 'it cried awful'. She admitted to not knowing what to feed the child on as food that was offered she would not eat. She described a bed that was made up for the child on the floor as there was no other place for her to sleep. She denied the testimony of the son Charles that she had sworn at the children when they arrived and stated that she had offered to leave Fellows in order that Mrs Fellows could return to the marital home and look after the children herself. One of the jury asked her why she had gone to the house in the first place, knowing that Fellows had a wife and children there. She answered that she went because Fellows had asked her to lodge there.

The coroner gave a lengthy summing up for the jury, stating that a case of starvation was a very difficult one to prove. The reason for starvation was either in not supplying food or giving food which the child was unable to digest. The jury only deliberated for a short while and then returned. The foreman stated that the verdict was that the child had died of starvation and that Fellows and Ratcliffe were criminally responsible for the death. The coroner asked for clarification, saying, 'Do you mean that they are guilty of the death of this child by murder or manslaughter?' The foreman, without any hesitation, replied, 'Guilty of manslaughter.' The couple were brought before the police court the following day after Sergeant Blacker had arrested them for manslaughter. When charged, Fellows said, 'No' and Ratcliffe stated that she was 'not guilty'. They were remanded for a week in order that the Public Prosecutor could be communicated with. The prisoners were charged that between 11 and 18 October they 'had feloniously and wilfully and with malice aforethought killed and murdered Annie Fellows aged 20 months'. The news about the terrible murder ensured that the funeral of the baby was well attended. Large crowds assembled at the cemetery in Maltby and Reverend Greenwood held the funeral service. It was not thought suitable for the two arrested people to attend, but the police were out in force to make sure that the peace was kept. On 5 November the pair appeared at the West Riding Police Court, but belatedly had just recognised the seriousness of their position and half an hour before the case was due to be held, had engaged a solicitor for their defence. Naturally, he asked for an adjournment in order to consult with his clients. The case was adjourned to Friday 8 November 1919.

The courthouse in Rotherham was crowded when the case was opened and the damning evidence was piled up against the couple. Evidence showed that little Annie was not fed even though the other children had received some food. She was not given anything as evidenced by the post-mortem results. The prosecution showed that the couple were jointly responsible for the death of the child but that the female prisoner was physically in charge of the child and therefore had both a moral and legal duty towards her to ensure that she received adequate nourishment and medical attention. The defence pointed out that one of the salient features of the case was that there was no malice aforethought and the prosecution had not produced any evidence to show a motive on the part of either of them, therefore there was no justification to send the accused to trial at the assizes for manslaughter. In fact some witnesses had said that the child was offered food which she had continuously refused to eat. The magistrates considered the case in private but when they returned to the court the chairman said that after careful consideration to points raised by the defence and the prosecution it had been decided that the pair would be committed to take their trial at the assizes.

On Monday 1 December 1919 the trial of Charles Edward Fellows and Emma Ratcliffe began and the hearing lasted all day. The evidence was given that the child was healthy until she went to live with her father at Maltby. Dr W J Candlish, the medical officer of Basford workhouse, said that when she was examined by him on entry to the workhouse she appeared to be a healthy and a well-nourished child. Other witnesses gave evidence about the ill-treatment offered to the child by Ratcliffe and that her cries of hunger were left unattended. Medical evidence showed that there was no food or water in her stomach, although the defence tried to say that the evidence of witnesses proved that she was walking around the day before she died and whether she could do that if she was so near to death. After a lengthy trial the pair were found guilty of manslaughter. Fellows was sentenced to six months' hard labour and Ratcliffe, thought because of her sex to be the main protagonist, was sentenced to nine months'.

This is one of the worst crimes that I have researched and I find that more could have been done by others to prevent the little girl's death. Mrs Fellows herself must have been aware that the children were not wanted by Ratcliffe and yet she took the children back knowing what kind of a reception was waiting for them. The neighbours saw the girl decline, but also did nothing to help her. If either had called in the police a young life might have been saved.

CHAPTER 7

Attempted Murder at Mexborough 1920

The crime of attempted murder is not always seen in the same light as the capital crime of murder itself. Nevertheless, the case that follows indicates that the attacker deliberately tried to end the life of his victim. The crime was committed with very little provocation and as a result of jealousy.

In the early part of 1920, John George Hollingsworth (27) of Dolcliffe Road, Mexborough, met and fell in love with a young widow named Elsie Shaw whose husband had been killed during the First World War, in October 1915. She was slightly older than him at 34 and had four children and a small widow's pension. In July 1920, Shaw got a job working at the pay desk of the Hippodrome in Mexborough. The couple had only been courting for a short while when he asked her to become engaged and she agreed. He became a frequent visitor to her house on Frederick Street, Swinton, where she lived with her children. In May, she saw him on the High Street at 9.00pm and he wanted to take her home, but she refused because she could see that he had had quite a lot to drink. Not wishing to be disturbed that night, Shaw locked up her house after being home only for a short while and went to a neighbour to spend the night, hoping that he would think that she had gone to bed and she would be left in peace. However, following a comment made by the neighbour, she changed her mind and decided to go home. There she found Hollingsworth in the kitchen. It seems that he had let himself in through some grating in the cellar where Shaw later found his pocket book.

The relationship had began to sour and by the beginning of October she decided that she had enough and broke off the engagement because of his jealousy; and because, as she said, 'there was no pleasure in his company'. A few weeks prior to this she also took in a couple of lodgers called Mr and Mrs Phillips. Shaw gave Mr Phillips the presents which Hollingsworth had given her to return to him. Naturally, Hollingsworth was not happy about this turn of events and he was heard threatening to kill her to several acquaintances.

In November 1920, Shaw exchanged words with another acquaintance, a Mr William Lee, and when Hollingsworth heard about it he went to her house and grabbed her by the throat, throwing her onto the floor. He then got on top of her, putting his knee in her stomach. Shaw, in an attempt to get help from the lodgers, kicked the brass fender which lay around the fire and Mrs Phillips heard the commotion and ran to her rescue. This brave woman picked up the fender and threatened Hollingsworth with it. Mr Phillips then came in and Hollingsworth left the house. Later that night, Shaw went to work. About 7.15pm she was in the pay desk at the cinema when Hollingsworth arrived and asked who was taking her home. She told him that she had already made arrangements to have Mrs Phillips walk her home. When she finished her shift at 10.00pm she and Mrs Phillips passed him once again in the High Street and she said 'goodnight' to him, but he did not reply. On 17 November, following advice from her brother-in-law, Mr Overend, Shaw went to the magistrates' court in Rotherham to take out a summons for assault against him. Hollingsworth had been told by Overend that she would be taking the summons out against him the day before and he was furious about it. He told Overend that if Shaw would change her mind he would never molest her again, but if she didn't he would 'do her in and himself also as he did not care if he lived or died'.

The following day, he saw Overend again and asked him if the case could be settled between the three of them out of court as he was concerned about his service pension as he felt that he would lose it if the matter came to the knowledge of the army authorities. Overend told him that he should have thought about that before. Hollingsworth shouted, 'I shall not lose my pension quietly.' He then went to see Shaw to get her to withdraw the summons as he did not want a black mark against his character. At 6.00pm on 19 November, he went once again to her place of work at the Hippodrome and once again asked her to withdraw the summons. With that he threatened her, saying that 'she would have to stand the consequences' and walked away. A little later, about 9.30pm, he again appeared at her work and put on the counter a silver watch she had given him, telling her that he didn't want it anymore. She could not reach it from inside the pay desk and he told her that if she came round to the front to get it he would not harm her. She told him that she was afraid to get it whilst he was there. He finally left, saying that he was going to the *Bulls Head* for a drink.

Following advice from the manager of the Hippodrome on the night of 19 November, she cashed her receipts early and left work at 9.45pm; and went to a dancing room in Cliff Street. There she met her brother-in-law who had expressed his concerns about Hollingsworth to the police constable and he escorted her home. Once again she passed Hollingsworth in the High Street. Overend went to see Hollingsworth to tell him that he had notified the police and Hollingsworth asked him if he knew about the disturbance at the Hippodrome. Overend told him that was the reason he had escorted his sister-in-law home. Hollingsworth said, 'All right, I shall do her in and somebody else as well.' Another worker at the Hippodrome, Lavinia Harrop of Wath Road Swinton, also saw the confrontation between Shaw and Hollingsworth and heard him threaten her, saying, 'I will finish you before morning.'

Having reached home safely, Shaw made herself some supper and then went to bed about 11.30pm. She slept soundly until she was woken by the feeling that someone was in her bedroom. Although the bedroom was in complete darkness she knew that it was Hollingsworth and was afraid. To try to deflect his anger she said, 'George I will marry you tomorrow.' He muttered something that she could not hear and grabbed her by the shoulders and punched her whilst she lay in the bed. She screamed for help and then saw that he had a knife in his hand and struggled to get it off him, receiving cuts to the hand trying to defend herself. Struggling for her life, she fell on the floor, suddenly experiencing a sharp pain in her left breast. She cried out 'Oh George let me alone I am finished', but he had not finished with her yet. He pulled some furniture behind the bedroom door as the Phillips's were now awake and trying to help the hapless woman. On the other side of the door the plucky

Mrs Phillips grabbed a poker and, forcing the door open, allowed Shaw to make her escape downstairs. Shaw noticed that a paraffin lamp that she had put out before going to bed was now lit on the kitchen table and in its light saw the nightdress that she was wearing was saturated with blood and she fainted. When she awoke she found herself at her neighbour's house.

Hollingsworth shouted down the stairs after her, 'If anyone interferes with me when I come downstairs I will split them down the middle.' Mr Phillips was in the kitchen when Shaw came down the stairs followed by his wife. Mrs Phillips saw that Hollingsworth was still holding the knife in his hand and that there was blood on it. Hollingsworth took the paraffin lamp and went into the cellar and in his absence they got the poor girl out of the house. Hollingsworth returned from the cellar with an axe. He asked Phillips where Shaw was and he told him that he didn't know. With that he knocked over the paraffin lamp, stating that he would 'set the b***** shanty afire'. Mrs Phillips bravely picked up the flaming lamp and flung it out into the street. Mr Phillips went to take the axe off Hollingsworth but he threatened him with it if he came any nearer. Hollingsworth went to a neighbour's house and asked if Shaw was there, but the neighbour, Mrs Robinson, told him that she wasn't. Shouting that he would 'go and finish the other b***** now', he put down the axe and left, still holding the knife.

A surgeon, Dr Phalla of Mexborough, was called to attend to Shaw's injuries. When he arrived at the house in Frederick Street he found her sitting at a table and noted her wounds were quite extensive. She was cut on her left arm, chest and face and there were two more wounds on the ring finger of her left hand; and many of her wounds required stitching. There was a superficial wound on her left thumb and left forearm. The wound on her chest was about 1¼ inches long and 2 inches deep. Another serious wound was on the side of her head, running right down to the bone which was exposed. He also noted that Shaw was shivering and suffering from shock. He visited her again at 10.00am the next morning and found her condition to be serious enough to have her removed to Montagu Hospital, Mexborough, where she remained until 27 November.

Police Constable Langton and Sergeant Dobson, hearing of the disturbance, went to Frederick Street, Swinton. On passing Brittain Street, they saw Hollingsworth and went to him, saying, 'What's the matter?' He replied, 'It's attempted murder. Lock me up', and at the same time holding out his hands for them to place handcuffs on. When they searched him they found a bloodstained sheaf knife in the right-hand pocket of his jacket and they noted that his face and hands were covered in blood. They took him back to Frederick Street and assessed the condition of Shaw with a surgeon in attendance. He was then removed to Mexborough police station where he was charged with attempted murder. In reply to the charge he said, 'Yes its murder I admit it.' He was taken to the cells and Langton returned to Shaw's house and found the bedroom in great disorder. Sheets and pillowcases were removed which were covered in blood. There was blood on the floor and the cellar grate had blood on the stonework. A nightdress was also taken and the bloodstained garments and bedding were produced as evidence in court.

On 20 November 1920 Hollingsworth was brought before the magistrate and the case was adjourned for the police to make further enquiries. The court resumed on 4 December. The first to give evidence was Dr Phalla who told the court that Shaw's wounds were very serious indeed and that she was lucky to be alive. He told them that if he had not attended to her so quickly there would have been serious repercussions. He told the magistrate that he had no doubt what so ever that the sheaf knife belonging to Hollingsworth was the weapon which had inflicted the injuries on Mrs Shaw.

Mrs Phillips told the court that she had lodged with Mrs Shaw for about seven weeks and that during that time Hollingsworth and Shaw had frequently quarreled. The neighbour to whose house Shaw was taken, Alice May Robinson, also reported an occasion when she had seen Hollingsworth sitting on the doorstep of the house on Frederick Street talking to Shaw who was in the kitchen. He was playing with his sheaf knife and she heard him say to her, 'This will be alright when I want to kill someone. I had this when I was soldiering and brought it back with me.' PC Dobson said that Hollingsworth had told him that if it wasn't for one of the children crying that he would have 'finished her off and then killed himself'. The magistrates had no option but to send him for trial at the assizes on a charge of attempted murder. Hollingsworth was brought into the court at the Leeds Assizes on 23 December 1920. The jury took no time at all to find him guilty and the judge sentenced him to five years' imprisonment, telling him, 'You made this life of this girl a living hell.' Hollingsworth did not respond as he left the dock.

Hollingsworth was lucky that the jury had found him guilty of attempted murder as if he had killed Mrs Shaw he would undoubtedly have been hanged. But on more than one occasion he had threatened to kill her in front of witnesses and did not try to cover up his actions. It has to be said that Mrs Shaw was lucky that she managed to evade being murdered by a man who was clearly under some kind of insane paranoia. Mental health problems were not fully understood in the 1920s and it would be years before such issues as paranoia or post-natal depression could be diagnosed and treated.

CHAPTER 8

Post-natal Depression 1916 and 1919

Pioneer Marie Stopes opened a family planning clinic in London in 1921 and was instrumental in bringing birth control to working-class people. However, it would be some years before such enlightenment reached the town of Rotherham. Nothing was known about the effects of post-natal depression, where women were expected to be the home-maker and child bearer, often resulting in year after year of pregnancies, leaving many mothers ill and debilitated, unable to cope. Although the condition was little understood, women who tried to end their own lives or their children's were generally dealt with sympathetically by the courts. But suicide during this period was an offence against the person until the passing of the Suicide Act of 1961. To take the lives of children by a parent indicates the deep impact that this kind of illness had on women, as these two cases will indicate.

By May 1916 the town of Rotherham was in the third year of the Great War. At a time when men were enlisting in their thousands little attention was paid to the women and their families that were left behind. Campaigns to raise pensions were made on behalf of the wives of soldiers and sailors, but the reality was that most women were left almost destitute and in sole charge of often quite large families. Alongside with the worries that the breadwinner may be killed, the fears of imminent invasion by the Hun and the bombing of the Zeppelins must have impacted on the mental health of some of these women. This next case involves another young woman with three children who, in May 1916, attempted to kill herself and the children in the lake at Clifton Park.

Clifton Park had been opened in June 1891 by the Prince of Wales, later King Edward VII. It was part of the estate attached to Clifton House and its beautiful grounds were a pleasure to behold. The park was central to the town and many events for inhabitants were held there, including civic celebrations, family picnics and sports meetings. There would be no reason to have concerns for the usual population going about its business on Monday 15 May 1916. However, thankfully, one man was concerned enough to watch a small family and due to his diligence he managed to rescue three children and their mother from drowning.

Arthur Marsden, who lived at Whybourne Grove, Rotherham, was walking through the park on that fateful day when he was passed by a woman and her three small children. Something about the woman gave him cause for concern and he later described her as looking 'troubled'. She was carrying a small child aged only a few months and two other children aged 4 and 5 were dragging on her skirts. When the young mother sat down at the other side of the lake, without really knowing why, Marsden also sat down and watched her.

The mother appeared to be in some distress as she contemplated the lake. To his horror, Marsden saw her suddenly leap up and, catching hold of the two eldest children, threw them into the lake. She then took the small baby into her arms and jumped in also. A man who was nearby witnessed what was happening and called to Marsden that he could not swim. Marsden, without hesitation, took off his jacket and jumped into where he had last seen the mother and the baby disappear beneath the water. He found them both about 8 yards from the edge of the lake and managed to pull them clear of the water. He then jumped in again and found the two older children who were about 12 yards from the edge and brought them safely to dry land. At this point a police officer named Sergeant Wilson, who had been taking a short cut through the park, arrived on the scene. He could see that the family was exhausted and the mother was semi-conscious and unable to stand. Wrapping the baby in an overcoat, he took them to a nearby shelter in the park and sent for Dr Anderson. When the doctor arrived he was concerned about the state of the little child and the behaviour of the mother. She was quite hysterical but nevertheless the constable had his duty to perform. He charged the mother with attempted murder, and she made no comment. Shortly afterwards an ambulance arrived to take the little family to the workhouse infirmary where they were cared for by the matron. Dr Anderson told the police that there were no serious concerns for the older children of the family, or for the mother, but he was extremely worried about the condition of the baby. He told the police that if Marsden had not been suspicious and watched the family, taking immediate action when he saw her throw the children into the water, then all the family would most certainly have perished.

It emerged that the mother's was name was Edith Thornton (36), the wife of a soldier, Private John Thornton, of Selbourne Street, Rotherham. Her husband had enlisted almost as soon as war broke out. She had struggled on for nine months on her own with the two children and a baby on the way and it is unclear whether her husband managed to get leave to see his new baby. Post-natal depression would have added to the woman's troubles, certainly it seems that she felt that she was unable to continue with the struggles of daily life. She had told the police sergeant that she had written a letter for her husband which she had left on the table at her home and, after consultation with the Chief Constable, Mr E Weatherhogg, officers were dispatched to the house to gain admittance and retrieve the letter. This is what she wrote:

> Dear Jack
> Forgive me but I feel I have not got the strength to battle with the children. You will find us in the lake. I have been up all night badly myself with all the children.

The following day, Edith was informed that her youngest child, John, aged 3 months, had died in the workhouse infirmary. The post mortem on the child's body revealed that John had been reported as 'chesty from birth' and undoubtedly this had contributed to his death. It seems that the baby had been only semi-conscious when it was pulled from the water and the jury took no time in recording a verdict that death was 'due to natural causes'. It was reported that the other two children, Edith (5) and Madge (4), were continuing to recover from their ordeal. The inquest was held at the courthouse in the town of Rotherham the following day, but Edith was in such a state of distress that the coroner, Mr Hastings, chose to discontinue the inquiry. He ordered that she be remanded for seven days and in the meantime she would be sent to Leeds where she would be able to have more specialized help.

Fortunately, her husband, had been sent for and was comforting her when the inquest was resumed. Throughout the ordeal she remained clearly distressed, resting her head on her husband's shoulder. The first witness was Arthur Marsden. He described passing the woman and said that his attention was drawn to her because she looked ill and depressed. He described the rescue to the jury, implying that the poor woman appeared to be in desperate straits. Her solicitor, Mr Gichard, no doubt trying to indicate her state of mind at the time, asked if he was prepared to say that she jumped or that she fell into the lake. But Marsden was not willing to swear to either statement. Mr Gichard again asked Marsden, 'Would you say that her actions in throwing the children into the lake were deliberate or impulsive?' but Marsden replied once again that he could not say. He did state however that the water was about 4 feet deep where she went in. When asked about other people in the park

Clifton Park Lake where Edith Thornton tried to kill herself and three small children. Rotherham Local Studies & Archives

that morning Marsden told him that from where she had been sitting she would have been very visible to many people who were taking the air.

Dr Lodge had visited Edith in the police cells after her ordeal, but she had been asleep and he noted that she had been tired and ill since the birth of the baby and was in poor mental health. He had been giving her medication for her health for the last four or five months. The jury had no option, given the evidence, for a verdict of attempted murder and the coroner then announced that Edith would be sent for trial to the Leeds Assizes. Her solicitor asked for bail but the coroner thought that she would continue to be cared for better at Leeds 'where she would have every care and attention'. As a consequence of this, bail was refused. Mr Gichard then asked for a certificate under the Poor Persons Defence Act, stating that the prisoner's husband, Mr Thornton, was now serving with the Colours and it would therefore be difficult for him to make arrangements for his wife's defence. The coroner agreed and the certificate was granted. The coroner then addressed Mr Marsden and said:

> I should like to take this opportunity in commending you for your bravery and the presence of mind which you displayed in going into the water and rescuing the woman and her children from what, without the slightest doubt, would have been their death. You must have the satisfaction of knowing that you have been the means of saving the lives of this mother and two of her children.

The trial was held at the Leeds Assizes in July 1916. The reporter stated that the prisoner appeared to feel her position keenly and was obviously under a lot of stress. When asked how she pleaded she replied that she pleaded 'guilty'. Once again the medical officer for Armley Gaol, Dr Exley, had observed her during her stay and told the court that he felt that she remained suicidal and depressed. He recommended that she was not to be left on her own and a constant watch had been made on her during her stay. The prisoner had her husband and her mother in the court room to support her. The judge, after listening to the medical advice, which stated categorically that to send her back to her life in Rotherham with the two children, would be inadvisable at that time. He felt that she had suffered enough following the death of the youngest child, but nevertheless justice had to be done. In sentencing her to twelve months' imprisonment he felt that she would receive the psychiatric help she so clearly needed.

★ ★ ★

Saturday 16 August 1919 was a beautiful day, just the kind when families would take a walk along the canal side. Such a family was walking down the towpath of the canal at Holmes, just on the outskirts of Rotherham. They consisted of Fred Barrowcliffe and his wife and child, from Ferham Road, Masbrough. Suddenly the beautiful day was shattered by a cry. Barrowcliffe noted a young woman had plunged into the icy water with a very young child in her arms which he estimated to be about 4 months old. He divested himself of his coat and waistcoat and jumped into the water where he managed to get the woman and child to the bank. Mrs Barrowcliffe meanwhile had gone to fetch a police constable. In an effort to calm the woman Mr Barrowcliffe spoke gently to her as he was extremely worried about the little baby who seemed to be unconscious in her arms. The name of the woman was Lillian Boyd (39), who

Ferham Road today. Chris Drinkall

The canal at Holmes where Lilian Boyd jumped in with four-month-old baby Fred Boyd. Chris Drinkall

was married, living with her husband and six other children in Harrison Street, Holmes. She told Barrowcliffe that she had intended to take her own life, saying that she 'had a lot of problems with a poisoned arm'. There was no sign of a constable and so Barrowcliffe walked her the short distance to her house. The policeman arrived shortly afterwards.

Barrowcliffe told the him that the child was still alive, but he was very worried as it looked in a very serious condition and so a medical surgeon was sent for. But by the time he arrived at the house the baby was dead. Boyd was by now quite hysterical but despite this she was arrested and charged with the wilful murder of her 4-month-old son Fred Boyd.

Lilian Boyd was brought before the police court on Thursday 28 August 1919. Throughout the enquiry she was reported as being very quiet. She appeared to be in a very confused condition. On the one hand she asked the constables in the dock, 'Where is my baby?' and then said, 'Isn't this a terrible thing to do?' but then said, 'It was the blood poisoning that did it.' The court heard the evidence of the witnesses and the surgeon and the jury had no option but to find her guilty of murder – and to send her for trial at the assizes.

The trial of Lilian Boyd was held at Leeds on 13 December 1919, where by now the poor woman had been assessed for the condition of her mental health. Evidence was given by the medical officer for the Armley Gaol, Dr Exley, who told the judge and jury that Boyd was debilitated by having seven children in nine years. The deceased child was born only eleven months after the previous child. Boyd had been unable to recover fully from previous births and suffered as a consequence from severe headaches, weakness, mental depression and loss of sleep. A local reporter from the *Rotherham Advertiser* reported that when Dr Exley examined her she asked him, 'Have I come here to die?' He tried to reassure her but she said, 'My only idea was to get out of the world and be at rest.' His medical opinion was:

> The prisoner, when committing this act, was the subject of acute melancholia and was therefore not of a sound mind. Her condition was aggravated by blood poisoning in the arm from which she was experiencing some pain.

The doctor's evidence was echoed by Mr John Clerk, the family surgeon, of Kimberworth Road, who had known the prisoner for quite a few years. He agreed that she was not of a sound mind at the time that she had jumped in the canal and gave his opinion that it was brought on by melancholia and a sense of unworthiness. The jury retired only for a few minutes before delivering the verdict of 'guilty but insane'. Boyd was sentenced to be detained at His Majesty's pleasure. Let us hope that, confined in some hospital, this poor woman found the peace that she so desired and which had driven her to commit this dreadful act.

Stories like these remained to be reported very often in local newspapers. The pressure of large families and the stressful conditions in which many of these families existed must have taken a terrible toll on mothers struggling to bring up children. It would be later into the century that birth control became more widely available and post-natal depression a recognized condition.

CHAPTER 9

Death of a Showgirl 1921

In January 1921, a scandal caused a sensation in the town when a man was charged with wilful murder following the death of a music hall dancer. The case shone a light on the murky world of music hall, abortion and fear of exposure. It started sometime in June or July 1920 when Robert Melville (40), made the acquaintance of a girl named Mary Taylor (24), known to all as May, who was performing at the Rotherham Hippodrome. May was a dancer from Brixton Hill, London and her costume was described as 'wearing a tall hat, a white Eton coat and black and white striped shirt'. Melville was described as 'French-looking, with a distinctive Scottish accent' and he was in lodgings at Clement Street, Kimberworth. They went out together but while Melville insisted that they were just good friends, Taylor told quite a different story. In July, she wrote to him from Manchester and agreed to meet him shortly as she was appearing in Keighley where they intended to spend the weekend together. On Saturday 17 August she met him at Keighley railway station at 2.30pm. He told her that he had never been to the town before, but he did know someone who lived there. He had a friend named Hiram Moore who owned a fish and chip shop and who had married a local woman. They managed to track down the

Robert Melville was described as 'French-looking' with a distinctive Scottish accent. Rotherham Local Studies & Archives

house where his friend lived but Moore was not at home. His wife went to fetch him and he expressed some surprise as he had not seen Melville since April 1919 but nevertheless welcomed the couple to his home. Moore later told the magistrate categorically that Melville introduced him to Taylor as his wife, although Melville denied this, stating that Moore had made that assumption for himself. The four people had some tea, then went to see Taylor's performance, returning back to the house later for supper. As it was now 1.30am Moore suggested that they stay the night instead of returning to Taylor's lodgings and they retired to the spare room. It was stated that Taylor 'readily acquiesced when this offer was made'. The following morning they arose at 9.00am and after breakfast returned to Rotherham, where Taylor continued on her journey to London with the rest of the troupe of musical halls artists. On the way to the station at Keighley Melville later stated to the court that Taylor had thanked him for the fact that although they had slept together, that intimacy had not taken place and thanked him for his gentlemanly behaviour. However, his later actions which led up to the death of Taylor disproved this assertion.

Melville had told Taylor that she could write to him and two or three letters had been sent to his place of work, the Rotherham Corporation Electric Power Station. To his surprise he received a letter in November stating that Taylor was pregnant and that he was the father. She told him that she had been ill and had consulted a doctor at Harley Street who had told her that she was pregnant. She was very distressed and told Melville that he would have to marry her, but Melville told her that he was responsible for his widowed mother and for the education of his sister; and was in no position to marry anyone. He told the court that he had asked her to keep the baby and he would have a member of his family take care of the child, but Taylor refused, as she would have to leave work, losing valuable music hall contracts. Taylor threatened that she would come to Rotherham and expose him or else she would drown herself or take poison, but she would not give birth to the child. She asked him to send her some pills which would cause an abortion and he obtained some and sent them to her. In fact he sent several lots of pills, but they had no effect and at this point she became quite desperate.

Rotherham Electric Power Station, 1920. Melville would have been familiar with this machine and possibly have known these two colleagues. Rotherham Local Studies & Archives

Taylor wrote to him in October, to ask if there was anyone who could perform an illegal operation on her as a relative had done this three times in the last fourteen months, and she understood that it was 'quite safe'. Despite his assertions that he wanted Taylor to keep the child, Melville wrote a letter to a friend in Glasgow, asking about a further acquaintance who appeared to know about abortions. He wrote:

29th October 1920

New Power Station,
Rawmarsh Road,
Rotherham

Dear Davy
I am in trouble. You can take it that I am giving you this distress signal even if you can't see me. Don't mention it to anyone but a certain lady is giving me to understand that

she is in a certain condition through me. I swear solemnly that it is not true, but that's not the point, Davy, she has put me in this mess and I have got to get out of it. Now I remember Rajah making a statement to me regarding his ability. Is he still in Glasgow? I hope to God he is and is as clever as he said otherwise as you can readily guess, I am ruined. Write to me if he can see me next week and I will run up to Glasgow and arrange with him.

Yours fraternally

Melville

Taylor wrote to him again once more, still very distressed, as she told him that she had tried unsuccessfully another suggestion to bring on an abortion. She had been advised to 'skip energetically' which despite undertaking this for as long as she could manage it hadn't worked. She was getting very desperate and once again asked him if there was anyone who could do the operation in Sheffield as it was a large city and there must be someone who could help her there. That way she would only have to take a week off work and have the operation done and no one would be any the wiser. Melville mentioned to his landlady, Mrs Mills, at Clement Street, Kimberworth, that Taylor was pregnant and although it wasn't his, he would help her out 'as a pal'. Mrs Mills stated that she knew a woman who lived on the same street, who had been known to 'help out' on such occasions, but she was not personally acquainted with her. She told him to leave it with her to make some enquiries and eventually Mills was introduced to this woman, Mrs Adeline Ashford Howard, by a neighbour, Mrs Sarah Ann Beever. On Friday 26 November, Melville told Mills that it had been agreed that Howard would undertake the operation and he asked her if she thought that £5 would be enough to pay. He also asked her if Taylor could stay at her house and Mills agreed providing that Taylor would have no objections to sleeping in her bed and she made Melville promise that the operation was not performed at her house.

Taylor appeared at the door of Melville's lodgings on 28 November. According to his later statement to the police he said that she had been present at his lodgings when he returned home for his supper and that Taylor and Howard were discussing the details of the operation. He ate his supper and then went to bed, wishing Taylor 'good night and good luck'. The operation was not straightforward however and between 30 November and 13 December Taylor left Mills' house to go to see Howard at Beever's house on several occasions. Mills categorically stated that she did not accompany Taylor on these visits but stayed at home. It became apparent that the ministrations of Howard were not working and there was some discussion about the strategies used. It seems that initially a syringe was used in an attempt to flush out the foetus with water and soap, as there was an enquiry at the inquest as to whether Melville had supplied the syringe, which he denied. It seems that more drastic measures were needed as there was also some discussion about using knitting needles which were too short and it was reported that Taylor gave Beever half a crown to buy some longer needles, but at the trial Beever denied that she had bought anything which might induce an abortion. Finally, on Monday 13 December, Taylor told Mills that the operation had been a success and she was waiting for the foetus to be aborted. Mills said that she had gone to bed at 11.00pm the previous evening, leaving Melville and Taylor downstairs after being requested to by Melville. She heard noises from the kitchen: 'bustling sounds, things being knocked about and high words'. At the trial she was asked why she didn't investigate the matter, but Mills said that when she became concerned that she had knocked on the door of her husband's bedroom, but there was no answer from him, and so she went back to bed. About 4.00am Melville came upstairs to tell her that the baby had been aborted. To the horror of the court she told how she had gone downstairs to make a fire in order to burn the foetus. Mrs Beever and Howard were called to the house and Taylor was finally put to bed about 5.00am and stayed in bed the following day. She came downstairs for a short while on the Wednesday but went to bed early that night and did not get out of bed again. It was on this day that Taylor gave Mills 5 guineas to give to Howard, which she did the next day.

By Friday17 December the poor girl was noted to be having a shivering attack and Mills wanted to call a doctor. At first Melville refused and then when it became clear that the girl was seriously ill he finally went upstairs and spoke to Taylor herself.

He told her that she had to say that she has used the syringe herself and had aborted herself saying, 'If the truth comes out I will get ten years for this.' He also told Mills, Beever and Howard to state that the girl had done this to herself and instructed them what to say if they were questioned. Dr Wildman arrived at Mills house at 9.30pm and immediately recognized that the girl was suffering from the effects of an abortion, sending Taylor into Rotherham Hospital. It was reported that when the doctor appeared Melville made himself scarce and left the house quickly. Taylor was operated on immediately but although she seemed to recover, septicemia had already set in. By 31 December it was obvious that the girl was going to die and she was asked to give a dying deposition at the hospital. The magistrates' clerk, George Clews, the Chief Constable of Rotherham, Detective Inspector Smith, Dr Fogarty, Taylor's brother-in-law, Herbert Edward Scott, the ward sister, Melville and Mr Aizlewood, a justice of the peace, attended her bedside in order to record her dying words. In front of all of them Taylor stated that she had been pregnant and that Melville was the father. She stated that she had asked Melville to marry her when she realized that she was approximately two-and-a-half months pregnant and he had refused suggesting that she 'get rid of her trouble'. She stated that she had been three-and-a-half months pregnant when the child had been aborted and Melville had done the deed in Mill's kitchen when everyone else had gone to bed. A few hours later the baby had been born and Melville had destroyed it in the fire, which had been in the kitchen grate. Melville had instructed her to buy a syringe, which she had purchased at Newport in Monmouthshire and she had been told to take it to his lodgings. Taylor admitted that the pregnancy had been as a result of one incident when she had been intimate with Melville at Keighley after she had a bottle of stout and she did not remember what took place. She stated that his friends had thought that they were husband and wife and they had slept together. Taylor said in the deposition that she had been extremely ill before going into hospital. She stated under oath and in the full knowledge that she was dying that she had not told her family about the pregnancy until a few days earlier and that she had gone to see a doctor (Dr Wyatt) at Harley Street because she was feeling so low and he had told her that she was pregnant. Melville stated that he had sent her a letter saying that she could not be pregnant by him, but she denied receiving such a letter. However, she did say that Melville had been very kind to her, but denied saying to him that if he wouldn't help her to have the operation she would drown or poison herself. In front of all these witnesses she emphatically stated that he had used the syringe on her, adding to Melville, 'You know you used the syringe.' Faced with such a comment, Melville said that he had declined to make a statement previously as he needed to shield two intermediaries. He also added that she was the instigator in the joint action.

Taylor died shortly after giving her deposition and the inquest was held on 22 January 1921. Melville attended with Mills and Beever and the sordid transactions were told to an undoubtedly shocked jury. Howard was also at the inquest, but as she did not have a solicitor the coroner advised her against giving evidence. Most of the statements made were contradictory as each person tried to put the blame on one another for this sordid murder. Melville made his statement saying that when Taylor returned from her visits to Howard she told him that 'the midwife had used a syringe'. On Monday 13 December he had gone to work as usual and on his return was told by Taylor that she had been to see the midwife again and that this time it had been successful. He sat up with her that night and at 4.00am the baby was aborted; and he was shocked and horrified to see that it was a fully-formed male child. He admitted asking her to tell the police that she had used the syringe on herself in order not to implicate anyone else in the crime. Then he destroyed all the letters he had received from her about the pregnancy, still maintaining that he was not the father of the child. He told the police that he had gone to the hospital to visit her on several occasions during her stay and she was always pleased to see him there. He was away from Rotherham from the 24–29 December and had arranged to visit her once more on the 30th but was prevented from seeing her by her-brother-in law, Herbert Scott, who told him that Taylor had made a full confession. She had implicated him in the murder of the child and he informed him that he was that he was going to be arrested. The next day he was taken to the hospital by the police to hear her dying deposition. He was questioned by the police but his answers were monosyllabic, consisting mainly of yes and no. Taylor said that he had been astounded at her allegation that he had performed the abortion himself and he emphatically denied telling her to buy a syringe. He stated that the only crime he was guilty of was aiding and abetting, but he was forced to by her threats of suicide and exposure.

Mills, who at first had denied everything, now told the inquest that she wanted to change her first statement and she repeated her involvement in the crime. She told the jury that Taylor had come to her house on 28 November stating that she was three-and-a-half months pregnant and had tried everything to abort the baby. She has also used a syringe on herself, but without any success. On another occasion she had asked Mills if she knew anyone who could perform such operations and she told her that Beever had been 'seen to' by Howard. Taylor asked her to make enquiries of Beever which she did. Beever next gave evidence and told the inquest that she was a married woman and lived near to Mrs Mills on Clement Street. Taylor had told her that she was in a situation in Doncaster and that her young man was not in a position to marry her. She asked Beever to speak to Howard to see if she could help. Beever said that she had spoken to Howard who agreed to meet her on 26 November. Howard did not appear to be happy about the operation and had used a syringe full of soap and water which she told her 'would not hurt anyone'. Taylor arrived at Beever's house on 29 November when Beever asked her if she was afraid she told her 'no'. Howard and Taylor went upstairs, but when they came down stated that they had not been able to manage but would try again later that same night. On Tuesday 30 November Beever went with Taylor to Howard's house but once again was unsuccessful. Later, after everyone had gone, Howard knocked at her door and told her that Taylor had been using the syringe on herself, but without any success. She was asked by Howard to get her a knitting needle and she gave her 2/6d to buy a long one, but Howard denied using such an implement on Taylor. On 16 December Howard again visited her and told her that Taylor was shivering and asked her to call on her which she did. She suggested giving her a 'warm composition' but Howard gave her brandy and water.

The coroner addressed the jury, saying that they were not trying to find anyone guilty at the inquest but to try to find who was responsible for the woman's death. It was obvious that she had died as the result of an operation, but apart from the deposition of Taylor there was no evidence as to who had done it. He felt that the evidence showed that the operation had been performed by Mrs Howard with the assistance of Mills and Beever. The jury had to decide what part Melville had played and whether the child that had been conceived was his. The jury found that Howard and the three women were jointly responsible for Taylor's death and were committed for trial at the assizes. After the inquest Melville and Howard were arrested and charged with wilful murder. Beever and Mills were arrested for aiding and abetting. Melville appeared to be in great distress and stood whilst the charge was read out with his head bowed. Howard was charged with manslaughter in that she did 'feloniously, wilfully and with malice aforethought did kill and murder Taylor'. She pleaded not guilty and the pair was sent to the assizes.

At the assizes in January 1921 the judge announced that the capital charge of murder was to be dropped and the charge against both Melville and Howard was manslaughter. Mills and Beever were discharged and Mills left the dock, but took her place amongst the prosecution as a witness. Herbert Edward Scott, a secretary to a variety agent at Brixton Hill, London, gave evidence that he had come to Rotherham on 30 December at the request of his wife who was Taylor's sister. When he saw her at the hospital she was very weak but she was clear minded in what she was saying. She told him that she wanted to make a statement and told her brother-in-law that her and the prisoners had done everything they could to bring on a miscarriage. He held her hand and was with her when she died. Then the two doctors appeared and they seemed to have different ideas on the lucidity of their patient. Dr W S Wildman stated that he felt that when Taylor realized the seriousness of her condition she 'could have been open to suggestion'. Dr Fogarty, the junior house surgeon, disagreed. He said that her temperature was 103 degrees and yet despite her fever she was 'sensible and didn't agree with everything that was being said to her'; and he thought that she was very rational in the conversations that he had with his patient. Moore told the court that when Melville introduced her to him he stated that she was his wife. The judge asked him, 'Did you make the assumption that she was his wife?' He categorically replied, 'No sir, he introduced her as his wife'.

In his summing up the judge stated that the statements of Taylor and Melville could not be relied upon as both had lied when it suited them. From the evidence it seems that the meeting at Keighley was made with the intention of spending the weekend with Taylor and she stated that they had slept together and intimacy had taken place. Melville had said that they had slept together, but no intimacy had taken place and yet he had agreed to help her out 'as a pal'. He also pointed out that Melville was willing to pay for the abortion but still denied that he was the father of the child. Mills had told them that between 14–16 December Taylor was very ill and she told Melville to send for a doctor, but he, after allegedly consulting with Taylor, told her that Taylor had not wanted a doctor to attend her. When the situation became so serious that a doctor had to be called Melville told her to say nothing about Howard and Beever and to say that she had done it herself. The judge said that when Taylor made the deposition she was in imminent danger of death and would view the matter as a serious one and he pointed out to the jury:

> One would think that she would tell the truth. If she had been responsible for her own condition she would hardly lie at such a time.

The jury considered the evidence for two-and-a-half hours before bringing in a guilty verdict for Melville and an acquittal for Howard. Melville was sentenced to eighteen months' imprisonment with hard labour. On 25 April 1921 he appealed against his sentence which, unbelievably, was quashed on the grounds that the judge had misdirected the jury by failing to instruct them to acquit him on the grounds that the only evidence against him was by an untruthful accomplice. Melville left the court a free man.

This sordid case indicates that lies were told on all sides. Nevertheless, an abortion did take place and the murder of a small child in such a terrible fashion surely meant that someone should have been held to account. The reasons for the lies were evidently to make themselves in a better light, but the dying deposition of the deceased should surely have been given more credence than it was.

CHAPTER 10

A Mother's Right to Defend Her Child

1922

On Sunday, 12 November 1922, Mr and Mrs Coley were at their home on Fitzwilliam Road, Rotherham having just finished lunch with their daughter Violet, aged 23, and two sons, Cyril (16) and Edward (9). Joseph Coley was 56 and his wife, Amy Selena, was four years younger. Coley had been subject to fits for the previous seven years and because of this was unable to continue his work at the Parkgate Iron and Steel Company; and subsequently had worked as a brickies labourer. The intensity of the fits caused him to be subject to bouts of instability and temper which he appeared to be unable to control. At 1.30pm the police were called to the house to find Mrs Coley hysterical and the body of Mr Coley lying on the floor of the dining room, having been shot by a revolver. He was still alive and an ambulance was called which took him to hospital. Chief Inspector Parkinson and Detective Inspector Clayton Smith questioned Mrs Coley who admitted shooting him. The gun was inspected and the police found that it was a six-chambered revolver, but only one bullet had been fired. She was taken to the police station and charged with the attempted murder of her husband. Crowds of people who had heard about the murder collected outside the house and witnessed the removal of Coley and the arrest of his wife. By the time she attended court the next day, Coley was dead and she was brought before a magistrate and charged with wilful murder. She told him that she had not meant to kill her husband, only to frighten him. The magistrate remanded her for seven days and the reporter noted that tears were streaming down her face as she left the court.

The inquest on Joseph Coley was heard at the Frederick Street Courthouse in Rotherham on Wednesday 15 November

Fitzwilliam Road in 1922, where Mrs Coley had worked before becoming ill.
Rotherham Local Studies & Archives

in front of the coroner Mr Bradford. Mrs Coley was still in custody, so she did not appear at the inquest. The first witness was an older son, John Arthur Coley (known as Arthur) who lived in Shakespeare Road. He told the coroner that he had identified the body of his father and admitted that the gun belonged to him. He had bought it at Nottingham in 1913 when training there for the armed service and had kept it with him until April 1916 when he returned home to the town. He was allowed to keep the gun under the Firearms Act providing he bought a license which he did, before giving the gun to his mother. He told the coroner that his mother was a hard working and respectable woman and all the family were regular attenders at Eastwood Wesleyan Church. Then the inquest was adjourned until the following Tuesday, 19 November, in order for more enquiries to be made.

At the resumed inquest Arthur gave evidence once again. He told the coroner and the jury that for many years his parents

Parkgate Iron & Steel Company, where Mr Coley had worked before his illness.
Rotherham Local Studies & Archives

had not been on good terms as his father frequently suffered fits, which led him to commit actions for which he was not responsible. The attacks became more frequent and he offered the opinion that his father was becoming more uncontrollable and dangerous. Arthur himself had intervened on many occasions when he became too violent. The police had been called to the house in January 1921 as he was threatening his wife and the children. He described one attack in the house when his father had broken both ends of the poker smashing at the furniture. Arthur had left the family home in 1921 when he got married and on one occasion his mother and the other children had to stay at his house during one of his father's uncontrollable moods. Three weeks before his death he had broken all the pictures in the dining room for no reason whatsoever. Arthur admitted being extremely worried about his mother for the last three weeks as she was becoming more scared of her husband and he was aware that she kept the gun close to her at all times, in order to be able to frighten him with it should he attack her or the children. Dr S W Drinkwater, the house surgeon at Rotherham Hospital, then took the stand and he told the coroner and the jury that he had been on duty at the hospital when Coley had been admitted at 1.45pm. He had tried to staunch the wound but was unable to stop the bleeding and the man expired at 3.15pm. He had undertaken the post mortem and found the entry bullet holes in the man's skull about 2 inches above the right eye. The bullet had exited out of the brain cavity and in an upwards position. He added that in his opinion death was due to the laceration of the brain by the bullet.

Cyril Coley, aged 16, told the inquest that his father had suffered from epileptic fits since 1914 and as a result of this had frequently shown great violence to all members of the family. He spoke of the events of the day to the courtroom, which was completely quiet, telling the jury that on the morning of the 12 November his father had gone downstairs about 12.30pm. He had been grumbling and complained at Cyril that he had not said 'good morning' to his father. Cyril went into the dining room about 1.00pm and heard his father telling Edward to go and change his jacket. Edward, aware of his father's mood, did so without further delay. Cyril said that he heard him coming down the stairs within about three minutes later, but his father had met him at the bottom and said something to him. Cyril did not hear what his father said but he heard Edward say, 'Dad, I was as quick as I could be.' Cyril went to the stairs where he saw his father grab Edward by the throat and shake him. Cyril went towards them and then his father started shouting at him, backing him into the dining room. He grabbed the poker from the fireplace and raised it into the air. His mother, who was at the back of the dining room, said something, although again the boy was unable to remember what it was. He then heard the shot and his father collapsed into a chair and he saw the wound in his head. Coley did not speak but fell from the chair onto the floor. His mother asked him to help his father 'as much as you can' and then cried out, 'I did not mean to shoot him' and handed her son the revolver.

Cyril was questioned by a juror who asked him if he had seen the revolver before. He said that it was not the first time he had seen his mother with the gun, and he was aware that she had kept it by her. He was asked by the coroner had he seen his mother point the gun at his father and he replied that he had when his father had threatened himself or the other children. In such circumstances when she pointed it at him, his father became quiet and calmed down. The coroner asked Cyril if he knew that the gun was loaded and he replied that he didn't know that the gun had been loaded at the time of the accident. He told the jury that his father was having more and more fits. The family could usually tell when they were coming on because he would start to mutter to himself as he had been doing on the day of the accident. Cyril stated that if his father had hit him with the poker he would have been dead. He had previously threatened him with some dumb-bells and if his mother had not intervened on that occasion, he was sure that his father would have killed him then. The family had lived in fear of him for four years. When his mother had threatened to leave him his father had told her that he would follow her to the ends of the earth if she did and he would kill her and the rest of the family.

Violet Coley took the stand next and she spoke about the fact that her parents had been very unhappy for the last four years. She had gone to Sunday school at 8.30am that morning and her father appeared normal to her and gave her no cause for concern. She had returned home about 12.40pm and found her father in the living room and her mother and Edward in the kitchen. She told the coroner that 'Dad had become quarrelsome and he had that wild look in his eye.' She was not in the room when the shot was fired but she heard it and went into the dining room. Her mother screamed at her to fetch the doctor and she went to the doctor's house, but he was not in. While she waited her mother arrived urging that the doctor come quickly to the house as her husband was in a very bad way. Eventually, the doctor arrived and they went to the house where her mother had now returned. The doctor saw that Coley was still breathing and he advised her mother to send for the police. Violet told the hushed courtroom that she confirmed what her brother had said that the revolver was the only thing that would quieten her father when he was in one of his rages. On one occasion he had attacked her mother with a knife and slashed her head so badly that she had required stitches. She spoke of another occasion when she came downstairs to find her father strangling her mother; she managed to intervene but her mother had marks on her neck for days afterwards. Her mother had been to see two doctors about her father's behaviour and had also gone to the police station on a number of occasions, asking for protection, but the police could not do anything about it as she refused to prosecute him.

Chief Inspector Parkinson and Detective Inspector Clayton Smith then gave evidence. They stated that they had arrived at the house at approximately 1.20pm and Mrs Coley was crying and stated to them that she did not mean to kill him. She was taken to the station and charged with attempted murder. She had made a statement saying that she had the revolver in her pocket and when her husband lifted the poker to strike at Cyril she drew it out, meaning to fire over his head to frighten him as she had done before, but the gun went off. She had not tried to aim at him, but the gun had just gone off in her hand. The police had then taken her to the hospital and she stayed with her husband until he died. He was unable to speak to her, but she was sobbing as she told him that she had not intended to kill him. On his death she was then charged with murder. The police told the coroner that in their opinion there was no intention to shoot him and therefore there was no 'malice aforethought'.

The coroner spoke to the jury and told them that in his opinion no one should keep a gun to threaten another person. If one man had shot another he had to take responsibility for his actions. The jury went to deliberate for fifteen minutes before they came back into the court room. The foreman said that they had the greatest difficulty in coming to a unanimous decision. They thought that it was an accidental killing and therefore was neither murder nor manslaughter. The coroner asked him, 'Did you mean it was an accidental death?'

'Yes sir, or it was a case of misadventure. The jury would like to express their sympathy for the rest of the family.'

The coroner interrupted him at this point saying, 'We should not bring sentiment into it.' He then warned them, 'I will take your verdict into account but if someone shoots another they are responsible for that death.'

At this point the foreman of the jury asked the coroner, 'Surely intention should be taken into account.'

The following day Mrs Coley appeared in the magistrate's court and the clerk read out the charge that she 'wilfully, feloniously and with malice aforethought did murder Joseph Coley on 12 November 1922.' The hearing took up most of the day with a large part of it on the question as to whether it was murder or manslaughter. The prosecution told the jury and the magistrate that

> they must take into consideration the fact that she had carried the gun around with her for four years. When the incident happened she was not being threatened and that when she fired point blank at him, the only conclusion had to be that of murder. Whilst no doubt he had every sympathy with the family in this case, a man is entitled to be as violent as he likes and he was still entitled to live out the rest of his life. The gun was fired and therefore the jury could not make out a case of accidental death.

The defence counter-argued that

> the family had offered every help to the police in this case and did not act like a guilty party. The prosecution states that the crime was one of murder but there was clearly no malice aforethought. While I recognize that the gun was fired not as a matter for self protection, but that it was an elementary principle of law that the act was committed to protect her children.

The difficulty in this case of proving the verdict dragged on until the clerk interrupted to state that in this instance it was not for the jury to prove the case but for a judge and jury to try it at the assizes. The magistrate agreed, saying that he had no option but to send her to be tried by judge and jury and therefore he would accept a verdict of manslaughter; and it was reported that Mrs Coley was once again crying as she left the court.

The case was heard at Leeds Assizes on 9 December 1922 and thankfully in this case was short and to the point. Before any witnesses for the prosecution could be heard the judge, Mr Justice Rigby Swift, told the jury that the law allows a woman to defend her own child and to use a deadly weapon for the purpose of preserving life. If the jury agreed then in that case they must record a verdict of not guilty. His Lordship spoke about his condemnation of firearms being kept in the home for any purpose, but in this case Mrs Coley could be forgiven, given the difficulty that the effects of the last few weeks have had on her. Questions were asked about what enquiries were made into a person wishing to keep a revolver in the house. He asked the Chief Inspector if he had enquired as to the reason that Arthur Coley had given for keeping the gun at home. He was told that the enquiries just took the form of enquiring into a person's character. His Lordship commented that 'It makes a farce of the law that if a man wanted a revolver and is of good character that he should be allowed to keep it.' The Chief Inspector had no option but to agree with him. The judge said, 'I recognize that it is not your fault, it is the system that is at fault', and the Chief Inspector, no doubt thankful, left the witness box.

The judge then asked the jury to retire and they consulted only for a few minutes before returning a verdict of not guilty. His Lordship said to Mrs Coley, 'You may be discharged and you may go free. I think the verdict of the jury is perfectly right. But you must never keep a revolver in your home again.'

Mrs Coley answered him, saying, 'Thank you my Lord. I don't think I will need one again.'

The judge replied, 'I hope you never will.'

It was reported that the whole case took only seventy minutes from start to finish as no doubt the joyful woman was released into her family's care. I like to think that such a case might not happen today. The police have stronger powers in domestic violence crimes than they had in 1922. Mrs Coley's reluctance to prosecute him, as every victim of domestic violence will know, was out of fear that it would make matters worse. But if she had the courage to go ahead it might have resulted in him being sectioned under the Mental Health Act and he might have been less of a risk to his family. We shall never know. I would like to think that the family lived the rest of their lives in peace and that they thought about the father as he was before the terrible affliction affected him to the extent that he obviously terrorized all those around him.

Chapter 11

Death on Gerard Road 1922

In the 1920s, very little was known about the treatment of epilepsy, despite the fact that it had been around for a long time. In 400 BC, the physician Hippocrates wrote a book stating what we now know to be true, that it was not a disease, but a brain disorder. But throughout the years the condition was little understood. European people thought that prayer could remove the fits which were caused by possession of evil spirits. Historically, people with the condition were shunned and often held in isolation as we see in our own royal family. Prince John, the youngest son of George V and Queen Mary, was kept in isolation, as it was felt that to acknowledge such a disorder would undermine royalty itself. Treatments available were either crude drugs or diets to reduce the epileptic seizures. In 1912, a treatment involving phenobarbital was introduced, which succeeded in reducing seizures for many patients. But generally speaking people suffering from this condition found it difficult to live a normal life and the effect on their families could be devastating.

There are some areas of Rotherham where wealthy businessmen built substantial houses in order to reflect their status and influence. These houses were generally larger to accommodate servants and the large families. Such a house was built on Gerard Road. By 1922, however, circumstances had changed and these large houses were no longer viable. The housing market was such that these buildings sold better when divided up into apartments with shared living accommodation. In one such house one apartment contained the Taylor family and another was shared by Mrs Thompson and her son, Hewan, a well-known concert artist. The Thompsons had lived at the house for six years. The Taylors, who previously had lived at the *Station Hotel*, Parkgate, had lived there for the same number of

Typical comfortable villas on Gerard Road. Rotherham Local Studies & Archives

years. Mr Taylor had found work at Steel, Peach and Tozer, but, following the industrial distress which was felt throughout Rotherham at that time, had been out of work since November of the previous year. The family consisted of Thomas Taylor (62) and his wife and three sons: Thomas junior, Albert Edward and William Vickers Taylor. There was also William's wife, Mary Elizabeth Taylor and a baby. It was reported that the two families got on well together.

Albert Edward had suffered from epilepsy which had been diagnosed not long after he was born. The seizures were thought to have occurred after a fall which affected his brain. For the last nine months his fits had been greatly reduced and it was thought that he might be able to lead a more normal life; but in the few weeks prior to April 1922 they had returned and been more ferocious in nature. When he was well he was regarded as a gentle and quiet young man. The return of his seizures was felt most strongly by his father, who became depressed and anxious about his son's condition. Due to his illness Albert Edward was unable to work and spent most of his time at home, looked after by his mother and father.

On Tuesday 4 April the day started off bright and sunny. The first to leave the house was Thomas junior on his way to work. He described how he had breakfasted with the rest of the family and that his father appeared to be his normal self, although slightly depressed, but giving no indication of the tragedy that was to come. Mrs Taylor, who also noticed nothing wrong, had decided to go shopping in Sheffield with a friend leaving her husband at home caring for his son. Albert Edward had had a serious fit the previous night and it was noted by both parents that each seizure seemed to take more and more out of him. When his brother and mother left the house he was lying on the sofa recovering. Mary chatted with her father-in-law in the morning and thought that though he appeared to be rather troubled, it was not enough to cause her to worry or think that anything about his demeanor was unusual. Mary had lunch with him and Albert Edward and left them in the breakfast room about 1.30pm to go for a nap.

Mrs Thompson went into the kitchen about noon to prepare lunch for herself and her son Hewan where she found Mr Taylor getting lunch for Albert Edward. He told her about the fit the previous night and how much it had taken out of him and that he had never been a strong boy; and that each day he seemed to weaken more and more. He said that it was a pity that his son's fits had started again and that he really thought that he would have grown out of them now. She later told the police that he looked very despondent as he said this to her, but she also felt there was no evidence that he was anything more than 'just concerned'. Shortly afterwards she went into her own sitting room where she remained until about 3.00pm when she heard a thud followed about ten minutes later by the sound of a baby crying. When no one appeared to attend to the baby she went to find Mary, the mother of the child. She walked into the breakfast room and into a terrible scene of carnage. Lying face down on the couch with his throat almost severed was Albert Edward. Kneeling at the side of him was his father with his throat cut also and next to him was a blood-stained knife. She later told the constable that there was blood everywhere. Mrs Thompson screamed and Mary rushed into the room where she saw the two bodies. In order to get help she ran outside the house where she found a passer by and begged him to come inside, saying that her father-in-law had killed his son.

Harry Lamb was unemployed and as he walked down Gerard Road about 3.20pm he noticed a young girl who he thought was hysterical. She told him that her father-in-law and brother-in-law were dead and he went into the house to try to find if there were any signs of life. He was taken aback by the bodies and the amount of blood. He knew that there was nothing he could do to help, but told Mary to phone for an ambulance. The house did not possess a phone, but the next door neighbours did have one, so she went there. Lamb stayed with the bodies and saw that there was no breathing from Albert Edward. When he touched the old man's hand however he murmured something but could not make out what it was. He waited at the house until the ambulance arrived. Police Constable George Henry Green and Police Constable Pratt arrived at the same time as the ambulance, which was about 3.10pm, shortly followed by Sergeant Northrop, who went into the breakfast room and examined the bodies. He noted that there was no sign of a struggle or anything broken. He found Albert Edward on the couch face down and his legs on the side of the couch, his life declared extinct by the ambulance attendants. Mr Taylor was on his knees at the side of his son and still breathing despite the large wound to his throat. The sergeant noted that the furniture in the room was undisturbed and the crime had been committed in a very short period of time. No doubt the thud which Mrs Thompson had heard was the father's body falling to the floor after he had dispatched his son and then himself. Mr Taylor was transported to Rotherham Hospital where he was given into the care of the house surgeon. The ambulance then returned to take away the body of Albert Edward which was taken to the hospital mortuary.

The hospital house surgeon, Dr Stanley Wilson Drinkwater, found that the father had slashed a wound to the left side of his neck which had detached the windpipe. He gave his opinion it had been self inflicted. There were signs of hesitation in the wound which confirmed this. On the body of the deceased young man the wound had been inflicted much deeper, penetrating the windpipe and large vessels on the left side of the neck. He was certain that in this case the wound was inflicted by someone else, as there were no signs of hesitation. A nurse was in attendance at the bedside of Thomas Taylor when he confessed to her what he had done. Nurse Mary Margaret O'Shaunessy told the police that she had heard the man state:

> I have murdered my son. He had a fit and I thought I would put an end to him. I don't want to live. Get the doctor to poison me.

Shortly after making this statement and exhibiting great signs of distress, a police constable arrived to sit by his bedside, but Taylor spoke no more and they were still there an hour later when he died. All the time that the nurse and the police constable were in attendance the man remained conscious and in great distress.

An inquest on the two bodies was held at the Town Hall on Friday 7 April in the presence of the coroner, Mr W J Bradford. The first to take the stand was Thomas junior. He told the jury and the coroner that he had left his father in good spirits when he went to work that morning, but hearing of the tragedy, returned home to find the bodies of his father and his brother in the breakfast room. The police, who were at the house, asked him to do a formal identification of the bodies which he did. He told the jury that his father had always showed the greatest affection towards his youngest son. Mrs Mary Taylor gave her version of events and agreed with the last witness that both the deceased were on good terms with each other and both very affectionate. Police Constable Green told the jury about finding the bodies of the two men and the only sign of the incident was a poker and a knife which had been on a table at the side of the man's body. Both of these implements were produced at the inquest. Dr Drinkwater was asked if Albert Edward had been conscious at the time that the wounds were inflicted and the doctor felt that as there was no sign of a struggle that in all probability he wasn't. The coroner asked if the wounds could have been inflicted whilst he was suffering from another fit. He replied 'quite possibly'.

The Old Town Hall, where the inquest on Thomas Taylor and his son, Albert Edward, was held. Chris Drinkall

The coroner summed up the case for the jury stating that there was no doubt that Mr Taylor senior had confessed to killing his son, making it clear what had happened. Nevertheless, it was the jury's duty to give a verdict of both causes of death. What they would be unable to do was to ascertain what state of mind Mr Taylor had been in during the crime on his son and they must decide whether he was in a state of insanity or whether it had been a deliberate act. It was for the jury to make up their minds. The jury only deliberated for a short while before returning a verdict that Mr Taylor killed his son, Albert Edward Taylor and then killed himself whilst being in a state of mind which was not responsible for his actions. The inquest, which had only lasted half an hour, ended with the coroner offering his condolences to the family of the two deceased men.

Crimes such as these could be prevented if they had access to the modern medication. Now most people with epilepsy can live normal lives providing they take the medication needed to stabilize their condition. Although it must be very distressing for parents to see their children having this condition, modern medicine at least brings the possibility of a epileptic being able to lead a normal life.

Chapter 12

Till Death
1936

Many of the cases in this book are of love tinged with jealousy, spilling over into murder. In the years before divorce became easier trying to get rid of an unwanted boyfriend or spouse was a difficult task and in extreme circumstances could end in tragedy. Sometimes people just won't take 'no' for an answer – as in this case, which fortunately for the accused resulted in attempted murder and not the full capital charge.

On 26 September 1936 a young assistant railway porter named Arnold Swallow (24), from Holmfirth, was charged with attempting to kill his girlfriend, Marion Prosser (23), of Toll Bar Road, Swinton. When he was arrested Swallow was found to have a gill-size bottle (about a third of a pint) of sulphuric acid, six twelve-bore cartridges and a newly sharpened penknife. The couple had been going out for over a year although Marion had tried to end it several times. Each time she did, Swallow threatened her and it was said that she only took him back because she was afraid of him. On Saturday 21 September Swallow went to her home, determined to speak to her.

The couple had met when Marion was working in domestic service at Honley, near Huddersfield, in April 1935. It was not a settled relationship as several times Swallow had used violence against her. On one occasion whilst walking in a wood he had pinned her up against a tree and tried to strangle her. This resulted in Marion having a large scratch to her throat which had been visible for weeks. After she broke off the relationship the first time, Swallow showed her a bottle containing sulphuric acid and wanted them to have a suicide pact; and he told her that if she killed herself first, then he would too. Fortunately, Marion was far too sensible and told him not to be so silly. Following a further row in September of 1935 he asked her to settle a motoring offence fine for him and said to her, 'If you settle this account for me, I will promise never to trouble you again and we can part as good friends. If not, just watch your step I warn you.'

Whether through threats or feeling sorry for him, she took him back again and the relationship continued. On Monday 21 September Swallow went to Marion's house where she lived with her parents and he asked to speak to her. Her father answered the door and told him to stop forcing his attentions on his daughter. On this occasion Swallow left, but the next day, seeing Marion and her sister, Gladys, walking to Mexborough, he caught up with them on the road and asked her if she really wanted to finish with him. She told him she did. He said, 'Don't forget what I said, TD. It is only 1936 now but you will never see 1937.' 'TD' was an abbreviation for 'till death'.

The following day, Wednesday 23 September, he went to the house of her parents again, but once again her father told him that he could not see her and closed the door on him. Refusing to go away, he sat on the doorstep from 6.30 to 8.30pm, waiting for her to emerge. When her father eventually came to the door and told him once again to go away, he refused once more; and when her father opened the door the next time he was still there. Through the open door he could see Marion and he shouted to her, 'Lets shake hands and remain friends.' Thinking that if she shook hands with him he might go away she went to him, but he pulled her towards himself and, producing a knife, slit her throat. She screamed and her mother, seeing what had happened, pulled her inside and shut the door in Swallow's face. The cut was 3½ inches in length and was a serious wound from which she was bleeding profusely. The police were called and Swallow ran away. A physician, Dr C J H Aitkin, was sent for and examined the wound. He wanted to put some stitches in it but Marion was nervous and refused. The following day she was seen by another doctor, Mr Panniker, who told her that she had to let him stitch up the wound or it would not heal. Reluctantly, she let him put in three stitches.

A warrant was put out for Swallow. He was spotted with a bicycle by two constables, Marooney and Sheard, the next day, at 10.50pm, in Blackamoor Road, Swinton. PC Sheard asked him his name and Swallow told him that he was John Smith of Griffin Street, Mexborough. He went to put his hand in his pocket but Marooney grabbed at his hand and pulled out the bottle containing the sulphuric acid. He was searched and the two constables found the cartridges and the penknife. On one of the cartridges and written in ink and inscribed 'to MP with love from Arnold xx TD' and on another one was written 'This is for MP'. They asked him again if he was Swallow and he replied, 'I have told you who I am.' They took him to the police station for further questioning. After some interrogation he was charged and he replied, 'Yes that's right, you have got me. I did it with that knife. When she screamed, I was frightened. I knew she would not die or you wouldn't have caught me.' The contents of the bottle were examined by Douglas William Auchinachie, who said that it was 88% pure sulphuric acid.

Swallow appeared in court on 7 October where he was defended by Mr Donald Dunn and Mr C Phythian was for the prosecution. A rambling letter indicating the turmoil of his thoughts was written by Swallow to Marion from prison and was read out to the court:

> Dearest
> I send this letter to you who I have hurt more deeply, so that I hardly know how to address myself. Believe me the task is more painful than the one I shrink from. However now the truth must be told and there is nothing in the world that will excuse my conduct. Would to God I had moral courage to open my heart to you and the world, but I could not bring myself to do so and now I know what a hopeless fool I have been towards you. Believe me from the very moment it happened, I have rued it, but I am quite aware that it is too late and I shall have to face it all. All I have done so far is to brood over you and I hope against hope that I have not hurt you as bad as I have thought.
>
> Yours ever, Arnold
>
> PS I love you.

Marion took the stand, the sight of the wound standing out in stark contrast to the paleness of her skin. She told the magistrate that throughout their relationship Swallow had often threatened to kill her if she finished with him or went out with another man. She was asked if she was planning to marry him at any time and she said that she had turned him down as she did not feel he was earning enough money to marry anyone. She was asked, 'Did you remember saying that if his situation improved she would marry him? but she stated that she did not remember saying any such thing. Asked point blank why she continued to walk out with him, she told the court that he had threatened her if she didn't and she did it to 'keep the peace'.

Mr Phythian told the jury that all the time that Swallow was sitting on the doorstep for a matter of over two hours, he was planning to murder Marion and therefore it was a clear case of malice aforethought. He had waited for the right time and brought a selection of weapons in which to carry out his task. Phythian also pointed out that the accused had told Marion on more than one occasion that he would kill her if she finished with him. There was, he said, clearly a charge of murder to answer for. Swallow's defence, Mr Dunn, pointed out that the evidence given by the two doctors indicated that the wound was not a severe one and the girl's life was never in any danger. He stated that the parents told him to go away and were well aware that he had threatened their daughter and yet they had often let him stay at their house. On a prior occasion he had stayed at the house overnight and they went away to Blackpool for the weekend. He suggested to the jury, 'Does that seem like she was afraid of him?' There was no doubt that Swallow regretted his actions and he read out a second letter sent to Marion in which he wrote:

> Dear Marion
> I have been thinking about you a great deal and wondering how you might be. I hope that you are recovering fast after what happened between us. If I could take back all that had happened, I would give my life. It's not that I am in any way ill-treated in here, no far from it, they are very kind. Have you received a letter I wrote to you, if so why have I not received an answer? Perhaps all the time we had means nothing to you. You are my only contact with solidity in this world of mirages. Please tell me if you would rather that I discontinued writing to you and I will retire gracefully. But I shall nevertheless remain yours with affectionate regard.
>
> Affectionately, Arnold
>
> PS Can you forward me a picture of yourself

Mr Dunn completed his case for the defence by asking the police authorities if, despite the cartridges, a gun had been found in Swallow's possessions, but he was told that it hadn't. The jury only took a short while to find Swallow guilty of attempted murder and when asked if he had anything to say he told the court that he was not guilty. Swallow was ordered to take his trial at the next assizes.

Swallow appeared at Leeds Assizes on 28 November 1936 and Marion once again gave evidence that she was frightened of him and only went out with him because he threatened suicide or that he would kill her. Swallow denied that he had any intention of killing her, pointing out that on the contrary he was extremely fond of her. The jury were not convinced and without retiring agreed that he was guilty. The judge, sentencing him to prison for five years, told him:

> After persecuting this young woman for a considerable time you finish up by a cruel treacherous attack upon her which only merciful providence prevented from being fatal. I have read the letters you sent to her from prison and to my mind they only show a degree of hypocrisy on your part which is shocking.

Without another word Swallow was led away to begin his prison sentence, showing no remorse for the attack on Marion. Once again it seems that there was some degree of mental disorder for such a jealous attack, but also, as we have already seen, it was difficult to diagnose or treat.

CHAPTER 13

The Gamekeeper's Revenge 1936

Poaching has traditionally been a way of putting meals on the family table at a time of year when food was scarce. It was seen as a working-class prerogative, by some, but as stealing by others. Poaching laws were developed to protect the property of landowners who could afford to pay keepers to ensure that any poachers were caught, brought before the magistrate and punished. Feelings were very high on the matter in the mid-nineteenth century on what was seen as yet another incursion on the rights of the working man. There was a lot of animosity between the poachers and the game-keepers employed to catch them, both parties going out armed with sticks to defend themselves. Some keepers felt that in the circumstances they could meter out their own kind of justice when they caught poachers.

John Unsworth (59) of Elizabeth Street, Hoyland, had been arrested several times for poaching and other crimes before he went out once more to try his luck on 19 October 1936. Accompanied by another man, Arthur Haigh, they walked along a pathway approaching Simons Wood, near to Brampton Bierlow, on the estate of Earl Fitzwilliam. Unsworth pointed out a cock pheasant and he went to the corner of the field to get a better view. In his pocket he carried a 'break-stock gun' which was in two parts and would need to be assembled before use. Before he could get it out of his pocket two keepers emerged from the bracken and attacked him. The two men were George Hall (28) and Harry Gale, both of Lee Cottages, Wentworth and both employed by the Earl as keepers. Gale lifted his stick and hit Unsworth across the face. Both men proceeded to attack him with their sticks; the gun he was carrying by now had fallen out of his pocket. Gale picked it up and hit him on the top of his head so hard that he knocked Unsworth to the ground and both keepers began to beat him again. During the attack Unsworth's false teeth were knocked out of his mouth. Haigh, seeing what was happening to his friend, ran away, convinced that if he showed his face they would attack him also. Finally, Unsworth shouted to Hall, 'For God's sake stop him, he is killing me.' Gale stopped beating him and told him to get up, but Unsworth was unable to do this without assistance. They pulled him roughly to his feet, warning him that if they saw him again they would have him arrested. Gale kicked him in the back to send him on his way and Unsworth staggered off.

For a second time the men came after him and told him to turn out his pockets and he was forced to hand over seven cartridges and some employment papers. They gave him the papers back and warned him again what they would do to him if they found him poaching and left him there. Unsworth, now walking with great difficulty, went to the nearest cottage and asked for help. His face was bleeding from the blows and he was breathing with much difficulty. The occupants of the cottage were so concerned about his injuries that they took him by car to the house of PC Ellis, who called in a doctor to look at his injuries. Dr Barclay Wiggins of Thistle House, Hoyland, found that Unsworth had been the victim of extreme violence and he had a cut on his head which needed eight stitches. The blows on his head had also penetrated to the skull and the kick on his back had damaged one of his ribs. He described him as being dazed and in shock, with bleeding from the nose and bruises around his mouth, eyes, chin, right shoulder and upper right arm. He had four scalp wounds and the rib on the left side of his back was fractured. The finger on his left hand was dislocated. He was asked by the magistrate what level of violence had been necessary to inflict such wounds and he replied that it must have been very severe and offered the opinion that it would have taken at least eight blows to inflict such injuries.

PC Ellis told Unsworth that he should make a charge against the two keepers for grievous bodily harm, a task which Unsworth did a few days later. Feeling more recovered, he went to the police station in Rotherham and made the charges against the keepers, Gale and Hall. Whilst he was there he was told that the gamekeepers had charged him with attempted murder. Inspector Marshall had been to his house to serve the warrant on him a day or so before but had found him ill and in bed, so he had not executed it. Marshall went to inspect the site of the attack and described finding the upper and lower set of false teeth on the ground. When the inspector went to serve the warrants for Gale and Hall, ther former had replied, 'I was only defending myself.' Hall had said, 'We have to protect ourselves.'

The two men were brought to the West Riding Police Court on 28 October, to be tried for the charge of poaching. However, when they faced the two gamekeepers, the latter now were telling a completely different story to the assembled court. They alleged that following some information which had come their way they went to Simon's Wood and hid. They then saw Unsworth and another man known as 'Midge' Haigh enter the wood, one of them holding a gun. The men under surveilence shot two cock peasants in the wood and both picked up the birds and put them in a paper container. When the two keepers emerged from their hiding place in the bracken, Unsworth, who still had the gun in his hand, reloaded, lifted it to his shoulder

West Riding Courthouse (right), where two gamekeepers were sent to the assizes on a charge of grievous bodily harm on poacher John Unsworth. Rotherham Local Studies & Archives

and pointed it straight at Gale, warning him not to come any further. Gale, who knew Unsworth as 'Trembling Lank', shouted, 'Put down the gun Lank' and in return Unsworth had threatened to 'blow Gales brains out'. Gale said to him, 'I am coming' and he ducked as Unsworth shot at him. He told the court that he had ducked, but felt the bullet fly past the top of his head and he claimed that he heard the whistle of the bullet. He told the court if he had not ducked there would be no doubt that he would be dead.

He then claimed that Unsworth tried to reload his gun but by now Gale was upon him and both men struggled, and the gun was finally wrestled from his hands. Gale told Hall to stand by as he could manage Unsworth on his own and admitted finding seven cartridges on him. Inspector Marshall saw Unsworth on 26 October when he took his statement and charged him with attempted murder. Unsworth denied the charge. The inspector told the court that in his statement he had not mentioned anything about shooting the two pheasants. Gale described the attack and stated that he had put Unsworth on the path and sent him on his way as he described how he had 'run off'. Mr Donald Dunn, who was defending Unsworth, told Gale that the statements made by the two keepers were 'A mass of lies concocted by the pair of them to hide the vicious attack which had been made on Unsworth.' The Dunn-Gale exchange went as follows:

Dunn: 'Did you know that Unsworth had complained to the police when you put in your complaint?'
Gale: 'Yes Sir.'
Dunn: 'Were you told that Unsworth was in a bad condition?'
Gale: 'Yes Sir.'
Dunn: 'And that he might die from his injuries?'
Gale: 'No Sir.'
Dunn: 'From a distance of 12 yards range he could have easily killed you?'
Gale: 'Yes, if I hadn't ducked he would have done.'

The questions continued about the attack and Gale admitted hitting Unsworth with a stick on his head but he was unable to explain the broken rib. He described Unsworth as 'running away from them' and that he looked like he had been in a fight. His face was all bloody and his head was bleeding. In his evidence George Hall told the court that he had not joined in with the attack because Gale had told him to stand back saying, 'I can manage him.' He described the way that Unsworth had pointed the gun at Gale and shot at him.

The questioning continued as follows:

Dunn: 'Did you take any part in the struggle and did you strike him at all?'
Hall: 'No Sir.'
Dunn: 'But you thought that Unsworth was intending to kill Gale?'
Hall: 'Yes Sir.'

Mr Dunn then told him that his evidence was 'a fabrication of wicked lies' and that there was no need for the attack after the gun had been taken away from Unsworth.

Dunn: 'Would you be surprised that Unsworth had to have eight stitches in the wound on his head?'
Hall: 'Yes Sir.'

He then asked Unsworth to bare his arm which he did to reveal the mass of bruises which were still visible. Hall told the court that Unsworth had said to Gale, 'I will get you next time.'

Unsworth described how he and Haigh had been walking along the footpath and the gun, which was in two parts, was in his pocket when the two keepers stood up about 2 yards away. He denied having shot any pheasants. He described how Gale had hit him in the face with a stick, knocking out his top set of false teeth and another blow which dropped him to his knees and it was at this point that the gun fell out of his pocket. Whilst on his knees Gale had hit him again and his lower set of teeth fell out. He tried to get up but couldn't and that was when Gale had kicked him in the back. He told the court that he was attacked by both keepers who rained blows on him. He was staggering away when Gale came up and took the cartridges out of his pockets. He knocked at the door of the nearest cottage and he was in such a state that the owner took him to the house of PC Ellis where he was told to make a charge against the two men. Mr Dunn pointed out at this point that if Unsworth had not made the charge of grievous bodily harm against the two gamekeepers that it was his opinion that 'nothing more would have been heard of this matter'.

In his summing up the magistrate stated that both Haigh and Unsworth had previous charges for poaching but, despite that, keepers were not allowed to attack poachers unless it was for their own protection. He fined Unsworth and Haigh 40s each for poaching and one month's imprisonment if they did not pay. Gale and Hall were sent to the assizes on a charge of grievous bodily harm against Unsworth.

Gale and Hall appeared at the Leeds Assizes on Thursday 26 November 1936. The court heard the story once again, but now there were other witnesses. Three schoolboys had been playing in the wood and had seen two men beating a third who was on the floor. They had become frightened and had run away. When asked if they had heard a shot, all three denied hearing any shooting at all that day.

The judge made his summing up for the jury but on this occasion they failed to agree a verdict.

A further trial took place on 12 December 1936 when it seems that the court was slightly more sympathetic towards the two keepers. Mr H B Hylton Foster, for the defence, said, 'Poaching was bad and wicked as well as being a nuisance to gamekeepers.' It was alleged that Gale had a 'terrible temper, so that he probably didn't know what he was doing'. Mr Willoughby Jardine, for the prosecution, said that Unsworth did not have a gun in his hands and he did not fire at Gale.

The two gamekeepers were found not guilty and were discharged.

This case typifies the difference of opinion that was around the subject of poaching. Some saw the keepers as being entitled to offer violence against poachers and the poachers saw shooting game as being part of their rights. There is no doubt that many gamekeepers would attack poachers to warn them off the land they were paid to protect and that no charges would have been brought. But it certainly seems clear, in this instance, that it was only when the charges were made against them did they concoct a defence of attempted murder.

CHAPTER 14

The Rotherham Trunk Murder

1936

This next case has all the ingredients of a good murder story: a body in a trunk, a national hunt for the missing killer, the calling in of Scotland Yard detectives and the first wireless broadcast for help from the public resulting in the murderer being found. But in this case it was a true crime, although the reason for it was never made public.

The case started sensationally enough with the finding of a young girl's body in a trunk at a house on Hartington Road, Holmes. Her name was Irene Hart and she had just turned 16. Irene had been previously been in service at the nearby house of Mr W D Jenkins of Ferham Road but had lost her job and was at that time living at home. She shared the house with her father, stepmother and her uncle, Ambrose Smith who was a severely disabled young man, practically bedridden. For the past four years, also living in the house, was the shadowy figure of her grandfather, known as William Smith, who came and went unseen by most of the neighbours. The house on Hartington Road was described as being semi-detached and had four rooms, two up and two down. The front room opened onto the street, but like many in the neighbourhood, the front door was rarely used, the occupants preferring to use the back entrance.

Irene Hart as a girl. Rotherham Local Studies & Archives

On the morning of 12 September 1936 Mrs Avice Hart put on her coat to go to the shops, leaving her father, son and daughter at home. She left the house about 9.30am to go into Rotherham. When she arrived back at the house, at approximately 11.00am, her father told her that Irene had gone out. Her blue coat was missing from its usual place at the back door and she asked her father where Irene had gone. He told her that he had given her some money about ten o'clock to buy herself a dress. Mrs Hart appeared to be a little concerned but her father stated that Irene had always said that she was going to leave home as soon as she could and he had no doubt she had taken the opportunity to run off.

The relationship between Mrs Hart and her father was a difficult one as he liked to 'rule the roost', as her husband Walter liked to say. By midday there was still no sign of Irene and Mrs Hart told her father that she was going to call the police. When he heard this Smith began to get agitated. Smith's wife had died about six years previously and he had inherited what he described as 'a suitcase full of debts'. Rather than pay them Smith went to live in Liverpool and the next time he saw his daughter she told him that a warrant was out for his arrest, for debt. He therefore did not want the police in the house and, putting on his jacket, told her that he was going to Sheffield and would be back later that night.

Mrs Hart went to meet her husband coming home from his work as a brickie's labourer for Rotherham Borough Council and she told him that Irene had gone; and that she wanted to call in the police. They both went up to the Irene's bedroom to find the bed made and no sign of a disturbance until Mrs Hart pointed out dirty handprints on a wall which had been distempered three weeks before. Walter noted that the closet door, which was normally closed, was open a fraction. He pushed it open further and saw that the opening in the roof to the attic was ajar. He got a chair and stood on it, gradually pulling himself into the attic where he lit a match. On the floor of the attic he found the missing blue raincoat, a handbag and a glove belonging to Irene, a red dress that she had been wearing and her knickers, which were torn. He handed them down to his wife, by now thoroughly alarmed, and without further ado Walter went to fetch the police. Mrs Hart, meanwhile, went back upstairs to the bedroom of her stepdaughter and looked around for anything which would give her a clue to her disappearance. Inside the closet was a tin trunk which Irene had used as a wardrobe and in which some toys had been kept. These toys were now on the floor. Lifting the lid, she saw some books and underneath she saw an arm. Rushing downstairs, she met her husband at the back door with PC Hoole and she told them what she had found. The police constable went upstairs with the distraught father to the trunk where Irene's body was found. She was wearing a blue petticoat which was torn and raised up to her waist and a blue jumper which was pushed up to reveal her breasts; and one stocking which was torn. A piece of cord was wrapped around her neck and tied with a reef knot.

PC Hoole called the station in Rotherham and more officers were sent to the house. The constable now made a thorough

The body of Irene Hart being removed from the house. Rotherham Local Studies & Archives

search of the house and found a torn eyelet from Irene's petticoat on the bedroom floor. Mr and Mrs Hart were then questioned about William Smith. Mrs Hart told them that her father made periodic visits to the house and that he was fond of his granddaughter to the point of possessiveness. In fact she told them that they had rowed recently over the fact that Irene had been to the pictures with another young uncle and a friend of his called Fred Lound. This had caused Smith to rant and rave about it, saying that she should not be seen out with two men, it wasn't decent.

Mrs Hart was asked for a description of her father which she gave and the information was passed on, stating that 'the police wanted him to help with their enquiries'. She told them that her father was

> aged 62, 5 feet 11 inches tall, well built, fair complexion, grey hair, no teeth and lantern jawed. He had an L-shaped scar on his left jaw and he might be wearing rimless glasses. He was wearing a raincoat, cord trousers and a dirty cap.

Mr Hart had been distraught at finding his daughter's body and kept breaking down as he gave his statement to the police. He told them he was 38 years old, a native of Parkgate and that he had married his first wife, Irene's mother, in 1918. They first went to live in Wortley Road where Irene was born on 7 August 1920. The couple then moved to Canklow Road where Mrs Hart died on 10 December 1930; and he had married his second wife the following April, moving to Hartington Road. The relationship between his second wife and Irene had been very good, in fact they had never been known to argue. He had trusted his wife's father to the extent that he slept on a mattress in Irene's bedroom. Irene had gone to Alma Road School when they lived at Canklow and then to Ferham Road Council School when they moved.

The house was thoroughly searched and in the kitchen was found a tub full of unwashed clothes. At the bottom of the tub was a piece of washing line from which the cord around Irene's neck had been cut. On top of the tub was an enamel bowl which when inverted acted as a lid. It was obvious at this stage that the murderer could only be someone who was familiar with the house and knew of the cord hidden in the tub. A pair of blue

Hartington Road today. Chris Drinkall

shoes belonging to Irene was found underneath the floorboards in her bedroom.

The inquest was held on Tuesday 15 September and there was a large crowd of onlookers outside the Rotherham Borough Police Court when Mr and Mrs Hart arrived. The coroner, Mr W J Bradford, told the jurors that the inquest was initially for the purpose of identification and to establish the cause of death, then it would be adjourned.

The girl was last seen alive at 9.30pm by her stepmother and when she returned at 11.00pm she was missing; and at 2.00pm her body had been found. The police surgeon had undertaken the post mortem on Sunday, the day after the murder, and told the jury that there were no external signs of injury, but the girl's mouth had been stuffed with newspaper and that she had been strangled. She was a very slight girl, being only 4 feet 9 inches tall. He admitted that the girl had recently had sexual intercourse, but there was no signs that violence had been used and, judging by the stomach contents, it was estimated that she had died between 10.00am and 1.00am on 12 September 1936. The heart was normal but the right side had been engorged with blood and the lungs contained dark blood. During the very short inquest Mr Hart was very distressed and was allowed to remain seated when he told the coroner that he had identified the body of his daughter. The coroner then adjourned the inquest to the following week.

The previous day, two officers were sent from Scotland Yard to Rotherham to help with the case. They were Chief Inspector Thompson and Sergeant Tasker and they spoke to the family and the county pathologist Dr Peter Lindsey Sutherland who had examined articles of clothing taken from the house. In an unprecedented move they ordered a search of every lodging house and every workhouse casual ward in the country, which took place simultaneously at midnight on Monday 14 September. It was known by now that Smith had used several aliases and was also known as Andrew Bagley. He had adopted the name Smith after living with a woman of that name. On Saturday 19 September, exactly a week after finding the body, a wireless broadcast gave a description of Bagley and asked anyone who spotted him to contact Rotherham Borough Police Office.

The curiosity surrounding the murder did not abate and hundreds of people were seen around the courthouse and the house itself on Hartington Road. Such was the public interest that the chief constable arranged for Irene's funeral to be held at Masbrough cemetery on the following Saturday, rather than the Sunday, in order to allow the couple to bury their daughter with dignity. Pictures of the funeral show Mr Hart in a state of great distress. There were some people who had been outside the house and had got to know about the re-arranged funeral, but they were kept out of the cemetery by the police, many of them having to watch the proceedings from the cemetery wall. It seems that this was a good move as the following day it was reported that thousands of people turned up at the cemetery to find the girl's funeral had already been held the previous day.

By 3 October there had been no sign of Bagley, although plenty of red herrings had been investigated by the police. A few days after the murder had been discovered, a body had been found in the water at Goole and one of Bagley's sons and a police constable were sent to see if they could identify the body, but it was not him. Sightings had been reported from places as far apart as Devon and Edinburgh, all of which were investigated. By now it was known that Andrew Bagley had been a native of Nottinghamshire, but had left that county forty years earlier. Prior to Wednesday 30 September it had been announced that Bagley was wanted 'to help the police with their enquiries' but after that he was 'wanted for murder'. It was also known that Bagley had kept two firearms under a floor-boards in the girl's bedroom. One of the guns was missing.

Finally, on 23 October, Bagley was spotted in a library in Hucknall, Nottinghamshire. A resident noticed him and felt that he fitted the description given by the police. Going out of the library, he saw Police Constable Sincham on traffic duty in the High Street and told him that he had recognized Bagley. Sincham went into the library where the wanted man was pointed out to him and he told Bagley that he was going to take him into custody. At first Bagley denied who he was when questioned by Inspector Healey of the Nottingham Constabulary, stating that he was Tommy King of Derby and he had no family and had never been to Rotherham; and had not heard of the murder. Just then another resident of Hucknall went into the police station and, seeing Bagley, said, 'I know you, we went to school together, your Andrew Bagley.' Faced with this identification Bagley had no option but to admit who he was. When Inspector Healey asked him about the murder he told him, 'I didn't do it and have nothing to fear, it's up to you to prove it.' Chief Inspector Thompson and Detective Sergeant Harper from Scotland Yard were sent to return him back to Rotherham. When they asked him to identify himself he told them that he was William Smith and had used that name for over forty years.

On 21 October Bagley was brought into the court room in Rotherham where he identified himself. The case was adjourned until the following week and it was reported that large crowds once again surrounded the police court but only a few spectators were allowed into the courtroom itself. Bagley appeared the following week but once again the case was adjourned to the following Thursday 12 November, exactly two months after the girl's body had been found.

The hearing of the case occupied the magistrates from 10.00am in the morning until 5.00pm and despite the rain many queued from 8.00am to enter the courtroom in which it was reported that 'many in the crowd were women'. Mr G R Paling appeared for the prosecution and Mr A H Jackson for the defence. Bagley was brought into the dock and soon complained that he couldn't hear the evidence and so was given a seat nearer to the Bench. The prisoner told the court that on the day of the murder he had booked a room in a lodging house in Liverpool using the name of Arthur Wilson. He had stayed in Liverpool until 23 October when he went to Hucknall.

Mr Paling started his case for the prosecution by stating to the jury that at the time the girl was murdered Bagley was the only one in the house, apart from the bedridden boy, Ambrose. In order to eliminate the boy Dr T V Griffiths from the Alma Road Institution (which was previously Rotherham Workhouse) had examined him and stated that he was an 'imbecile and stunted in growth with the strength of a child of 6 years of age 'and that 'he was unable to walk or get out of bed without assistance'. Two witnesses, a neighbour, Mary Evans and a 12-year-old boy collecting sticks called Charles Smith, had stated that they were within sight of the back door for the crucial hours whilst Mrs Hart had gone out and that no one had come in or gone out of the house apart from her. To cover up the crime Bagley had taken the girls coat up to the attic to make her stepmother think that she had gone out. His fingerprints were found on the enamel bowl in the kitchen, consistent with him having lifted up the bowl to get the cord. His fingerprints were also found on the knife which had been taken up to the bedroom to open the trunk as this was the only way of opening it. Evidence that would only be known to someone who was familiar with the layout of the house.

The first witness was Mrs Avice Hart. She told the jury how Bagley would stay at the house for a night or two on a regular basis but then for the last three years he had lived with them permanently, but always avoided being seen coming or going from the house. She knew that Bagley was intending to buy Irene a dress for Christmas but was surprised when he told her that he had given Irene a pound to go to a nearby shop called the Cosy Corner for a dress and a band for her hair. She described going into the house and seeing him looking 'dirty and wild'. Later, he said to her, 'She won't come back, the first opportunity she gets she will go.' When she told him that she was going to call in the police he donned his raincoat saying, 'I will go to Sheffield and I will come back tonight.' When asked if Bagley had ever gone out before in daylight she stated that that he hadn't. After finding the clothes in the attic she told the magistrates that she had gone back into Irene's bedroom and noticed a part of a blue underskirt hanging out of the trunk; and that's when she lifted up the lid and saw the girl's arm. On Saturday 29 August Irene had gone to the pictures with two young men, one her uncle and the other was a young man called Fred Lound. When Bagley came back to the house and heard that Irene had gone to the pictures with the two men he lost his temper shouting, 'It's not right, she should not have gone to the pictures with them. She was his girl and no one else's.' Mrs Hart described how her father had gone to the knife drawer with the intention of 'doing himself in' but she intervened and stopped him. She said that she lived in fear of her father due to his bad temper.

Mr Hart next appeared and told the court of his relations with his father-in-law which was very difficult as 'he always saw himself as the gaffer'. Mr Hart described how Bagley was always causing rows in the family. He described meeting his wife in Sarah Street and after she told him that her father had said that Irene had gone to the Cosy Corner shop they went to find her; but there was no sign of Irene and the owner told them she had not seen her. He went back home with his wife and she told him that her father had gone out. He spoke about the night Irene had gone to the pictures with his younger brother called Harold and another young man called Fred Lound; and the three young people arrived back at the house at 8.00pm. The prisoner had gone

Pavilion Picture House, where Irene, Fred Lound and her uncle, Harold Hart, went to the pictures and which so upset her grandfather. Rotherham Local Studies & Archives

into the yard and then stormed back into the house in a temper. He had shouted at the two young men saying that they were 'To leave her alone as he was there to protect her.' Mr Hart told him to shut up as he had enough of him; and the young men went to leave. Irene escorting them to the bottom of the street.

Mr Harold Hart, the brother of Mr Hart of Hollybush Street Parkgate, told the court about going to the Tivoli Picture House with Irene and Fred Lound and on their return being shouted at by the prisoner, saying that it wasn't right that two men should go out with one girl. When Harold returned the next day to see his brother he found Bagley in Irene's bedroom. Bagley talked to him for about an hour and apologized for his behaviour the previous evening. He told Harold that he had six revolvers under the floorboards of the bedroom and showed him a wallet with about £40 inside. He also had some letters addressed to Irene which he said were about jobs. Harold was aware that Irene at that time was looking for a job, so assumed that's what they were about.

The next witness was Frederick Garden, the owner of the lodging house at Byrom Street, Liverpool. He told the court that on the day of the murder the prisoner had booked a bed in the name of Arthur Wilson and had stayed until 6 October. He described the clothes that the man wore, which were different to those given out by the police. When asked if the prisoner had carried a raincoat he said, 'He hadn't seen him wearing one.'

PC Hoole described going to the house with Mr Hart and told the court how he lifted up the lid of the trunk and found books in it and he could see beneath them a part of an arm. He gave the books to Mr Hart and the body of a young girl was revealed wearing a blue jumper and a blue underskirt. He found the girl to be dead so he closed the lid of the trunk. He found a knife on the wash stand near to the bedroom door which had been used to open the trunk. When searching the room carefully he found Irene's shoes under the floorboards. When questioned by the jury foreman he told him that the shoes were not found directly under the floorboards but about 'an arm's length into the middle of the room'. He found a small metal eyelet which matched the material of the girl's blue underskirt. Later he swept the floor and put the contents into a clean envelope for the pathologist, Dr Sutherland. At this point the case was adjourned until the following day.

Detective Sergeant Harper was the first witness the next morning and he told the court about taking a statement from Bagley at Hucknall when a point of law was raised. It seemed that Harper had taken the statement from Bagley before arresting him for murder but just informing him that he 'was wanted for questioning'. As a consequence of this oversight the magistrate had to seek advice as to whether the statement could be read out in court. Other members of the bench agreed that it could and the statement was read. Bagley told him that Irene was to be married at Christmas and a young man called Tom had called at the house on the day of the murder. He had gone to the front room leaving the two young people alone. He said that he saw Tom leave the house about 10.30am and was under the impression that Irene was with him. When he left the house he saw a report of the murder and claimed to be 'astonished' and then he left for Liverpool. He stated that he

> had been as good as a father to Irene and I have practically kept her for the last four years. I thought the world of her.

Bagley was found guilty by the jury and the magistrate sentenced him to be tried for murder at the assizes. The jury at the assizes agreed and, following his trial on 5 December, also found him guilty. When the clerk of the court asked Bagley if he had anything to say as to why the court should not now pass the sentence of death, Bagley replied that he 'was not guilty' in a very loud voice. The clerk placed the black cap on the judge's head and the latter pronounced the death sentence. Bagley then swung around and walked unaided down to the cells, exhibiting no sign of emotion whatsoever.

Clearly the relationship between Irene and her grandfather was a curious one to say the least, but no doubt he was trusted by the girl's father enough to allow him to sleep in her bedroom. We shall never know exactly what went on to 'tip him over the edge' but the relationship was not a healthy one and there is no doubt that jealously was involved.

CHAPTER 15

Malice Aforethought 1939

When juries are making a decision in a murder case they have to decide whether the murderer actually planned in advance to carry it out. This was termed 'with malice aforethought' and the only verdict had to be one of murder. If someone was being attacked and defending themselves, leaving the attacker dead this was not seen as being premeditated and therefore it was judged to be manslaughter. In this case the victim, although suffering from murderous attack from her husband, nevertheless waited until he had gone back to sleep before attacking and killing him. This 'cooling off period' gained for Annie Bell a verdict of murder, before thankfully reducing it to manslaughter.

Annie Bell (50) was a married woman and by the beginning of July 1939 had led a very tempestuous lifestyle with her husband, John Horace Bell (54). The man was known to be violent and had several times attacked his wife; and on more than one occasion had tried to strangle her. They had been married for twenty-four years and the attacks were becoming more frequent, exacerbated by his drinking at the weekends. They had moved house several times and one son had left home due to the constant arguments and beatings. They had lived at Henry Street, Masbrough, where the eldest son, also called John Horace Bell (22), had been to the police station on many occasions to complain about the treatment that his mother received at the hands of his father. He had seen marks of violence many times on his mother's face and body and on at least three occasions had to intervene when his father tried to strangle her. His father appeared to take a dislike to his son for defending his mother and also threatened him with his fists. The situation was so bad that in the end he went to live with his sister (19), and her husband, Mr and Mrs Dorothy Steer, at Drummond

Street. They had become tenants of the property in April 1939 and had a young baby, but were happy for him to stay with them and escape from the many family rows. His mother, father and two children, Norman (15) and Desmond (4), then went to live at Rotherview Road; but matters were just as bad and shortly after this he was joined at his sister's house by his mother and two younger brothers. In the middle of June 1939 he returned home to find his father at the house and the rows had started all over again. The family shared the middle bedroom which had two double beds in it. One was occupied by Mr and Mrs Bell and the other by the two younger children.

Bell was the kind of man who, as the old saying goes, 'could fall out with himself in a room on his own' and was particularly incensed when his wife asked for money. He took objection to his son, also called John, eating meals, despite the fact that he was regularly giving his mother 26s a week for board and food. On 1 July the elder Bell came home drunk at sometime between 8.00pm and 9.00pm. The house was empty apart from his wife and before long they were engaged in a struggle. He pushed her onto the floor at the top of the kitchen steps and then he hit her in the mouth, breaking her false teeth. He tried to strangle her with his hands around her neck and she had to plead for her life. He threatened her with a poker from the kitchen and she ran upstairs to bed. When he came into the bedroom he started to swear at her, calling her what she described later as 'dirty names'. Eventually he calmed down and before long she could tell by his breathing that he had gone to sleep.

In her first statement to the police, Annie stated that she went downstairs to the cellar and picked up a hatchet and, taking it into the bedroom, hit the sleeping man several times on the head. She then threw a coat over her nightgown and went outside, where she saw a man passing and asked him 'to go and fetch a bobby', saying, 'I have killed my husband.' Another woman called Mrs Booth was passing along Drummond Street about 10.30pm when she heard Annie telling him to fetch the police. She went across to comfort her. Annie told her that her husband had been trying to strangle her. PC Hearn arrived at 10.40pm and Annie told him that she had killed her husband, stating that she had 'done him in'. Hearn asked her where the body of her husband was and she told him in the middle bedroom. He went upstairs to see the man who was lying on his left side and his head was covered in blood, his body covered with a blanket. Going back downstairs, he saw a bloodstained hatchet lying on the kitchen table. A police ambulance was called and Bell was rushed off to hospital where he was admitted with extremely serious head wounds. PC Hearn noted that although he could tell that Annie had been drinking, she was by no means drunk. Annie was taken into custody and when Detective Inspector Thompson told her that her husband was in hospital and 'they had reason to think that she was responsible', she answered:

> Wouldn't you have done it if you had been me? You know what I have had to put up with. He had been drinking all day and it was his ill-treatment which made me do it. He has been like this for the past twenty-four years. He loves me when he is sober, but always knocks me around when he is drunk. He asked for all he got and I am not sorry for it.

Thompson had no option but to charge her with attempted murder. She was then examined by the police doctor who saw a bruise on her eye and other bruises on her neck consistent with the grip of a hand. Detective Thompson was called to the hospital at 8.45am on 3 July, to be told that Bell had died at 7.30am that morning; and he then returned back to the police cells where he informed Annie of her husband's death and that the charge was now wilful murder. Annie was taken into court the same day where she appeared before the magistrate, Mr W Brooks OBE and was remanded for eight days. She was accompanied by a police constable and a police matron. It was reported that she appeared rather nervous, but composed. She had another brief appearance in court on 11 July when the case was adjourned until 21 July 1938.

The trial took place with Mr Donald Dunn defending and Mr E G Robey for the prosecution. The first witness called to the stand was Annie's eldest son, John Bell who described the rows and the time he had found his father trying to strangle Annie, banging her head on the floor of the bathroom. He had stopped his father who then threatened to fight him. When asked if he was afraid of his father, John admitted that he was when he had been drinking which was usually every Saturday and Sunday. He told the court that on many occasions he had to sleep on the settee downstairs so that his mother could sleep in his bed. He described to the court the events of the last day of his father's life. His father had returned home from the pub at 2.45pm. His mother had blacked his shoes, ironed him a shirt and put out his studs and a fresh collar ready for him to change into. His father, when he saw these objects, asked her, 'What the hell have you done that for?' She told him that she wanted him clean and tidy for the cricket match. His father started to eat his dinner that his wife had prepared for him and she asked him for some money to buy Norman, the 15-year-old, some clothes and he told her that Norman had enough clothes and complained that she 'skinned him to the penny'; he then threatened to do her in. John told the court that his mother had once tried to take out a maintenance order against her husband on the grounds of persistent cruelty but the application was dismissed and she had no option but to continue to live with him.

A neighbour was next called who said that she had heard the sound of rowing from next door between 8.00 and 9.00pm and she also heard a knock but she didn't know what it was. Mrs Booth gave her evidence regarding seeing Annie at her door and asking a man to fetch the police as she had killed her husband. She told the court that Annie had said that she loved her husband, but 'he went out with other women'.

Dr Thomas Victor Griffiths, the police surgeon, said that he went to the house and examined the bedroom at 11.30pm. He found brain tissue in the bed and on the floor and blood splashes on the wall on the right hand side. He saw the prisoner at midnight at the police station and she was agitated and distressed. On the right side of her head were red marks which were consistent with manual pressure and further recent contusions on her right eyebrow. On 3 July he completed a post mortem on the deceased man. He found a compound, committed and compressed fracture of the skull on the left hand side. There were extensive lacerations of the brain tissue and broken parts of the skull which had been driven into healthy tissue to a depth of 2 inches. He had several scratches on his neck caused by fingernails. One blow from the hatchet would have caused death but in his opinion there had been at least two blows. The scratches on the dead man's neck were consistent if he had his wife on the ground and was attempting to strangle her and she was trying to prevent herself being strangled. Detective Robert Thompson said that when charged Annie replied, 'I did it in self defence. If I hadn't done it he would have killed me. Wouldn't you have done the same?' When he further charged her with murder at 8.55am on 3 July, she replied, 'Yes sir, I did it.' The defence added that he did not expect to call any witnesses for her defence at that stage nor did he intend for her to give evidence herself. The magistrate had no option but to send her for trial for murder at the next Leeds Assizes.

On 4 December 1939 the trial of Annie Bell began and the above witnesses gave their testimony. When it was time for Annie to take the stand she presented as a downtrodden woman looking much older than was her age. She told the court that she had been married for twenty-four years and her husband had made her life 'a living hell'. She had never had a holiday, nor had her children, and she was not allowed to do her own shopping. Interestingly, new facts began to emerge and her story had changed. Annie told the court that she was attacked by her husband and when she got him into bed he finally fell asleep and she got out of bed to go downstairs and he heard her and sat up saying to her, 'I will finish you.' She picked up the hatchet which by now was at the foot of the bed, since her husband had recently used it to mend the bed, and she hit him with it. Then she covered him and went downstairs, putting the hatchet on the kitchen table where it was seen by PC Hearn.

The jury took just over an hour to bring in a verdict of guilty of manslaughter, the foreman adding 'under great provocation'. The jury also added a strong recommendation for mercy. In sentencing her to twelve months' imprisonment for manslaughter, Mr Justice Oliver told her:

> I am very sorry for you. You have had a dreadful time. The jury has come to the conclusion that you struck the blow in anger and under great provocation, but in sentencing you, I cannot ignore the fact that you have taken a life.

After the trial, Annie's daughter, Mrs Dorothy Steer, sent a message to the judge thanking him for the outcome. She said to reporters, 'My little brother is only 5 and is living with me now, but he is always asking where his mummy is. We have told him that she is in hospital because we are trying to shield him from the truth.'

It was later announced that a petition had started for an early release date for Annie Bell from a former neighbour in Henry Street who had a tailor's shop. He had known her for many years and it was reported that he 'has a book in which signatures are invited'. I found no evidence of whether Annie left prison early or whether the petition had been successful, but it is to be hoped that it was. Certainly the second statement made to the court differed in many respects to the first. If it had been proved that she had gone down to the cellar to pick up the hatchet, she would clearly have been found guilty of murder. The reason for the change in story is not explained but what was evident is that she suffered at the hands of a violent and brutal man for many years. In these inter-war years of the twentieth century women still had no recourse to a way out of such a grim existence and had no option but to endure it.

CHAPTER 16

The Body in the Ditch 1940

By 1934 there were many more cars on the roads around Rotherham than in previous years. A family saloon cost somewhere between £150–£350 in 1930 and for many motorists easy terms were offered making the cost of a motor car available to more families. The *Highway Code* book was published in 1931, offering guidance and rules for drivers following growing concerns over the rising toll of motoring deaths. Compulsory driving tests were not brought in until 13 March 1935, so prior to this only a rudimentary knowledge of driving was required. The ease with which people could travel also was realized and the days of the travelling salesman were becoming more in vogue. Not only was it more convenient to be able to travel distances, calling in at local branches with the firm's products, but carrying a selection of goods was easier via the boot of a car. One such travelling salesman was accused of causing the death of a pedestrian near Bent Laithes Farm, Whiston, in February 1934.

Mrs Sylvia Stevenson Hinchcliffe was fond of playing golf and would often be found playing a round or two at the Sitwell Golf Club, where she was a member with her friend, Mrs Nellie Seymour. Mrs Seymour, who had known Sylvia for many years, and was described as being a close personal friend, received a phone call from Sylvia on the morning of Wednesday 14 February at her home in Hounsfield Road, Sheffield, asking her to call in to see Sylvia and they would travel to the golf club. Mrs Seymour caught the bus to Whiston and arrived about 1.00pm. She stayed for something like thirty minutes before Sylvia drove them both to the golf club. Sylvia had been ill recently and was still feeling weak but both women felt that the air would do them good. They played a round in the monthly Medal Competition and then Sylvia drove herself home where

Bent Laithes Farm. On this deserted road witnesses identified the car at the time of the death of Mrs Sylvia Hinchcliffe. Rotherham Local Studies & Archives

it was agreed that Mrs Seymour would call in before catching the bus back to Sheffield. She duly arrived at 4.45pm where she only stayed long enough to smoke a cigarette and chat about an engagement that Sylvia had that evening, before catching the bus home, totally unaware that she would be the last person to see Sylvia alive.

Sylvia's body was found the next morning by Ernest Clayton Walker, a train fireman, of Toll Bar Road, Listerdale who was walking to work at 7.00am. He was passing the farm when he saw the body in a hedge bottom, on the left hand side of the road. He described the clothing as clean and undisturbed, apart from a fur coat which was twisted up at the back. She had been wearing a white silk scarf which he said was over her face, but other witnesses claimed that the scarf was around her neck and her hat was over her face. Her face was all bloody on the right side. He assumed that she had been knocked down by a car and looked around for any sign of damage from a vehicle, but found nothing. Her hands were cold and she was wearing a wristwatch which he said had stopped at 7.30pm. Again another witness stated that the watch had stopped at 8.45pm. Mr Walker saw two men approaching who said that they were labourers on their way to work and he asked them to stay by the body until he could call out PC Wright who resided at Woods Foot Farm. PC Wright went back with him to where the two men were waiting and saw the body which was covered in frost, making it obvious that it had been in the ditch for quite some time. PC Wright went to a nearby house opposite, telephoned the police station at Rotherham and was told by the superintendent to go back to the body and not disturb it but to look for anything that might indicate how she had died. He found a hair slide about 12 feet from the body and half a pair of spectacles, 16 feet from the body. The other half of the spectacles were found later.

The county pathologist, Dr Lindsey Sutherland, was next at the crime scene. He found nothing in the position of the body or clothing that would indicate that this was a robbery. Her underclothing had not been disarranged in any way and he confirmed that the woman was dead. The body was removed and a post mortem carried out. Dr Sutherland found that death was caused by a dislocation at the base of the neck, lacerations of the brain, haemorrhaging and severe bruising of the right shoulder. In his opinion the wounds were consistent as if she had been hit with some heavy blunt instrument such as a car. An inquest was arranged for the following day, 16 February, in front of the coroner, Mr C N Roberts. Dr Sutherland established that the cause of death was the fracture at the base of the neck. The victim's husband, Percy Wilkes Hinchcliffe, attended the inquest and confirmed that he had identified his wife's body on Thursday 15 February at the mortuary in Rotherham. He said that he was concerned the previous night when he arrived home and his wife was not there but he assumed that she had stayed the night at a friend's house. His supper was waiting for him when he arrived home and he was not unduly concerned, although his wife usually left a note if she was away for the night. He said that his wife had been in ill health and had difficulties breathing and for that reason he had bought her a car. During his statement to the coroner, Mr Hinchcliffe appeared to be very upset and distressed. The coroner then made a statement that a man had been arrested and charged with the manslaughter of Mrs Hinchcliffe and the police had requested that the inquest be adjourned until more enquiries could be made.

The man who had been charged was Frederick John Briggs (26), a travelling salesman for a firm of tailors, and he was brought to the West Riding Police Court on Tuesday 20 February 1934. From enquiries made, the police had established that Sylvia had left home about 5.30 to 6.00pm on the Wednesday evening, which was described as being very dark and overcast. Briggs was defended by a Sheffield solicitor, Mr William Mitchell, who told that court that Briggs had called at a house at Bentley Road, Bramley and left a few moments later to drive to Sheffield. He had both headlights and sidelights on but admitted that the headlight on the nearside was faulty, throwing the beam of light more towards the centre of the road that the edge. He was driving about 25mph and had traveled about 50 yards past the crossroads when he felt as if someone had thrown a stone at the windscreen. The windscreen had cracked and he got out of the car and went back along the road to see if he could see what had caused the problem. He had called 'hello' but could not see nor hear anything. He got back into his car and carried on with his journey. He put the car in the garage when he got home and thought no more about it till later the next day when he heard that a woman had been killed and a photograph of the stretch of road was in the newspapers. He knew that was the road where his windscreen had cracked. When he inspected his car, he found the front wing of the mudguard buckled which he had not noticed the night before. He voluntarily went to the Sheffield police station and gave a statement to Superintendent Thomas Woodward.

The post-mortem findings were confirmed by Dr Sutherland who stated that on the right side of the deceased woman's head was a large scalp wound about 5½ inches from back to front and about 2½ inches wide. There was a fracture at the base of the skull and marked lacerations of the brain. On the top of the right shoulder a large yellow brown bruise was seen as well as lacerations on the left knuckles. The cause of death was the fracture, lacerations of the brain and hemorrhaging. She must have been hit with something very violently and would have died instantly. Following a question from the coroner he stated that she had not been run over and her hat had no blood on it when it was examined.

Dr James Mathewman Webster, the Sheffield City police surgeon, attended the police station at Sheffield on 16 February and examined the saloon car belonging to Briggs. On the left-hand door he found three bloodstains but could not estimate how old they were. On the nearside top of the windscreen he found the cellulose work was braised and covered with a number of fibres. He later noted a tear in the deceased woman's hat and thought it might have been made by the windscreen. He could not say without a microscopic examination whether they were from the hat but the fibres could not have been imprinted on the cellular part of the windscreen without a heavy blow. The car was also examined by Duncan Stewart, a man who worked at the Rotherham Car Company and who had thirty years' experience of working with cars. He found the nearside lamp had been torn away from its contact with the wing and a dent was seen in the wing of the car. A wire was broken from under the headlight and in his opinion he thought that it had been done recently. The front end of the bumper was bright as if it had been rubbed and the windscreen was cracked from the centre to the nearside pillar and the paint had come off. The handbrake was good but the ratchet would not hold and the foot brake was only moderate and the application of it would not stop the car. The nearside headlight was loose and was inclined to point to the offside and very little light would be seen to the front or near side during darkness. It had already been established that the night had been a dark one, so his evidence was particularly damning. Had Briggs run Sylvia down without seeing her? It was certainly thought by the court that driving a car in such a dangerous condition was foolhardy and bound to end in an accident at the very least. But in his statement which he made voluntarily Briggs did not mention to the police any problems with his car on the night in question.

Two other witnesses were heard who had been on the road near to the farm that night. Francis Aylward and his brother William were waiting for transport back to Doncaster at 6.00pm. They had been working at laying cables and were waiting for their lift with a good view of the road to the farm. Francis described hearing a bump and saw a car with its headlights on come to a standstill and a man get out and look at the back of the car. When questioned as to whether he had heard a shout he told the court that he had heard nothing. After a minute or two the car had driven away with the lights switched off. He said that he thought that something had fallen off the car. He was asked in which direction the car was going and he said the car was going towards Sheffield. His brother, William, corroborated his evidence.

Mr William Mitchell made a spirited defence of his client when he told the court that in this case they would have to prove that the car involved in the accident belonged to Briggs and also to establish that he was driving it at the time. He told the jury:

> The case as it stands rests on minute fibres which Dr Webster states that with the naked eye looks like that might appear to belong to the deceased woman's hat. Apart from that there is nothing whatsoever to connect Mr Briggs with the lady's death.' There is little damage on the car and the bloodstains could not be established as being fresh. No one saw her on the road that night and the sad fact was that people get killed on the roads with regularity. Even if the accident was caused by Mr Briggs, it could have been purely accidental. It was up to the prosecution to make a case against him and they would have to prove the he was driving negligently.

The jury disagreed and Frederick John Briggs was formerly committed to the assizes, charged with manslaughter and dangerous driving.

The trial was set for 16 May 1934 when it would seem that the jury agreed with Mr Briggs' defence and Mr William Mitchell's conclusions. With only a short consultation with his colleagues, the foreman of the jury found Mr Briggs not guilty of manslaughter and also not guilty of driving his car in a manner dangerous to the public. The jury, which consisted of eight men and four women, did not even leave the court to consider their verdict. The hearing had lasted for just over four hours. Mr Justice Finley stated that he was aware that the woman had not been well for some time and they will never know the reason why she died. It was known that she was wearing high-heeled shoes and it was possible that she might have fainted. He told Briggs, 'I am satisfied that you are not guilty of causing the death of Mrs Hinchcliffe'. Briggs was then discharged from the court.

Unfortunately as time went on more and more accidents were noted by cars and only with the introduction of compulsory driving tests were drivers forced to become more efficient. By 1960 MOT testing was introduced on all cars over ten years of age to ensure that brakes, lights and steering were checked every year. It would seem that Mr Briggs was ably defended by his counsel and that he was just in the wrong place at the wrong time.

Chapter 17

The Unfaithful Wife 1941

John Broddle had lodged with Mr and Mrs Jackson at their house on Sandringham Avenue, Whiston, for seven years before receiving his call-up papers in April 1941. The Second World War had been raging for almost two years, with the decisive moments of the Battle of Britain just a month away, which many people saw as the beginning of the end of the war. Broddle had joined the Army during Easter 1941 and returned on Friday 18 July on his first leave home. The couple and their lodger were on friendly terms, although Frank Jackson had in the past suspected that there was more than friendship between his lodger and his wife. But when he asked her she always denied it and without sufficient proof he decided to forget about his concerns.

On Saturday 19 July Jackson went out, leaving his lodger, his wife and two children, Hilda (12) and Margaret, who was always called Peggy (6), in the house. At about 3.00pm Jackson was returning home and met Broddle, in his uniform, near to the Whiston crossroads. Broddle told Jackson that he was going to see his mother at Laughton. When he got home Jackson found his wife and the two children getting ready to go out also. She told him that she was going to see her sister at Handsworth, Sheffield and they were going for a picnic. As a consequence the children were very excited. After they had all gone out, Jackson noted Broddle's civilian jacket on the back of one of the chairs and a corner of an envelope popping out of a top pocket. Pulling it out, he saw that the note was in his wife's handwriting but it was addressed to Broddle. By now thoroughly alarmed, he read the letter, finding evidence that his wife and Broddle had been having an affair as she wrote to him in very affectionate terms. She called him 'my own darling, darling sweetheart' and 'husband mine' stating that 'she couldn't wait to be in his arms

Whiston crossroads, where Jackson met his lodger, Broddle, before going home and making the shocking discovery of his wife's affair. Rotherham Local Studies & Archives

again'; and she spoke very disparagingly of her husband. Looking through the rest of his lodger's clothing, he also found a telegram addressed to her telling her that he would be home that weekend and ending 'yours truly John'.

In his statement to the police he told them that by now he 'was seeing red' and searched through all Broddle's possessions, where he found two more very passionate letters and one revealing the biggest shock of all: that the youngest child, 6-year-old Peggy, who was his great favourite, was not his child but had been fathered by Broddle. When he read this letter Jackson broke down and cried at the betrayal of his wife and his lodger. Gathering the letters and the telegram, he decided to find his wife and confront her with the evidence, but catching the bus to Sheffield he found his wife's sister ready to go out and she told him that she had not seen her sister for over a week. There had been no plans for a picnic and she had no idea where her sister was at the moment. Jackson showed her the evidence and she was amazed as she had always thought that relations were very good between her sister and her husband. Leaving his sister-in-law's house, Jackson returned to Rotherham and searched for his wife in Clifton Park and the fairground but he could not find her. He later told the police that he had gone into a public house in the town, but had only had a glass of mild beer to calm him as he was becoming quite agitated.

Jackson returned home about 8.15pm, still upset, as he sat and thought about his wife and the lodger's betrayal and contemplated what to do. His state of mind was such that he decided that he was going to kill them both and tried to think about the best method. He had nothing in the house with which he could do this but he remembered previously having borrowed an axe from a neighbour to cut up sticks. He went to his neighbour's house and asked to borrow the axe again. His neighbour, a woman called Mrs Flaxley, gave it to him and later told the police that she had heard him chopping up wood. He then took the axe into the house and put it down at the side of his chair where it could not be seen by anyone coming into the room. He then went into the village and bought his wife two bottles of beer which was what she usually drank before going to bed. When questioned later, Jackson said that it was to try to make his wife think that everything was normal, but inside, his mind was racing. About 9.45pm his wife and children arrived back home. She stated that she felt unwell but managed to drink some of the beer, while her husband planned what to do next. He had thought earlier about challenging his wife, but wanted to do it while Broddle was there and to face them both. Broddle came back to the house about ten o'clock when both children were in bed. Although he was sober he appeared to Jackson to be in a bossy frame of mind and seemed to be taking charge of the house. He had brought some sausages and he gave them to Mrs Jackson, saying to her, 'Look at what I have brought you. Then he made some remark 'about being a lucky chap and they both laughed'.

He told the police in his statement that Broddle's attitude caused him to pick up the axe and aimed it at his head shouting, 'You b***** dog. You have wrecked this home, so take this', and hit him with the sharp edge of the axe. Jackson later told the police that he was very dazed and could not recollect how many times he hit Broddle, but he knew it was more than once and that he intended to kill him. His wife screamed and got hold of his arm and he said in his statement 'that steadied me'. She shouted, 'You have killed him Frank' and I told her, 'It serves you right for the game that you have been carrying on.' She then took the axe away from him. Broddle was still conscious and said to Jackson, 'You have killed me Frank. This is a nice way to spend my weekend's leave' but Jackson said, 'You deserve all you got.' Whilst Broddle was still conscious Mrs Jackson told her husband that she loved John and that they were going to find somewhere to live together. A neighbour, hearing the screaming, came into the house and, seeing Broddle on the floor, picked him up and put him into a chair; and then went to call the police and an ambulance. By the time Broddle was put in the ambulance he had lost consciousness. PC Studholme arrived at the house and Jackson gave him the axe and the letters, and admitted to attempting to kill Broddle. He was taken to Rotherham West Riding police station where he was charged with the attempted murder of John Broddle on 19 July 1941. Broddle was seen by Dr George Maschanzker of Rotherham Hospital who saw the serious condition of the victim. He felt that Broddle might die at anytime and inspected the three serious wounds to his head. Despite the terrible wounds, Broddle recovered and was discharged on 13 August, in order to be sent into a Northern Military Hospital for an operation.

Frank Jackson was taken before the magistrate on Wednesday 27 August. It was reported that he was soberly dressed in a dark suit and white shirt and appeared to be quite calm. He was defended by Mr J P Crehan and he pleaded not guilty to the charge. His neighbour, Mrs Georgena Flexley, took the stand and she told the court about the night that Jackson had come to borrow the axe. When questioned, she said that he had appeared normal and because he had borrowed that axe before and returned it, she had thought no more about it. She said it was about ten o'clock when she had first heard screams and ran to the house next door where there was a great commotion. Mrs Jackson was screaming at her husband, 'You have killed him' and Broddle was on the floor with his head covered in blood. The children were standing at the bottom of the stairs and crying, so she took them both back to her house. When they got back to the house Peggy asked her, 'Has Frank killed my daddy?' and she didn't know what to tell her. She told the court and the jury that she had always found both Mr and Mrs Jackson to be a very nice couple and good neighbours. Her husband corroborated her evidence, stating that as long as he had known Jackson he had always been a very quiet man who appeared to work hard to maintain his family to the best of his ability. He had not known anything about the affair between Mrs Jackson and their lodger and commented that 'they always seemed to get on very well together'.

The prosecution was undertaken by Mr R C Linney who told the court that he had read the letters which were not just affectionate but passionate, leaving him with the conclusion that Mr Jackson was justified in his claims that his wife had been unfaithful with Broddle. He mentioned that any man reading that his youngest child, who he had always thought of as his own was not his, would have been very upsetting. The letters also spoke of the prisoner in tones that was very dismissive of her husband which must have goaded him when he read them. He told the jury that he did not intend reading the letters out in court, but added that it was very clear that the couple were indulging in an illicit affair. One sentence from the letter written by Mrs Jackson read, 'I want nothing more than you.' The letters left no doubt in his mind of the relationship between Mrs Jackson and Mr Broddle. PC Studholme told the jury that when he saw Broddle sitting on the chair at the house 'he was in a soldier's uniform which was covered in blood at the front and back of his jacket'. Mr Jackson stated that he did not know why he had done it but that he had done it and gave him the axe stating '. . . and this is what I did it with'. He was taken to the police station at Rotherham where his statement was taken. When the statement was read out to him Jackson asked if he could add something and wrote at the bottom in his own handwriting:

> It's the truth I have told, the whole truth. I am sorry I did it. It was because of what he had done with my wife

The jury took only a short while to bring in a verdict of guilty of attempted murder and Jackson was sent for trial at the assizes. When the question of bail was discussed he was told that if bail was granted that he must not try to contact his wife or Broddle and he would have had to go to the police station every week. He told the court that he was intending to go to live with his father to Wombwell and try to get a job in the colliery there; and he added that there was no question that he would not turn up for trial, but the magistrate after consulting with others agreed not to let him have bail 'in case of another attack as it was in his own interests to keep him in custody'. He was then led away.

Frank Jackson appeared at the assizes on Saturday 6 December 1941 and Broddle was the first witness. He spoke about the attack and said that he had always been on friendly terms with Jackson but told the judge that he was madly in love with Mrs Jackson and she was with him. When the judge asked him what his intentions were towards Mrs Jackson he told him that 'after certain proceedings' he was going to marry her. Jackson appeared to be unmoved by this statement. PC Studholme spoke about the night of the murder when the prisoner told him that 'the minute he went down I regretted what I had done'. When Jackson took the stand he repeated that he had never meant to kill Broddle but that his blood was up and he just found the axe in his hand. Mr Linney, on behalf of the prosecution, asked him, 'Would you have hit Broddle again if your wife had not took your arm?' and Jackson admitted that he wouldn't and when he felt her hand on his arm it had steadied him and he realized what he had done. However, he pointed out to Jackson that in his statement he said that he had argued with Broddle, whereas in actual fact Broddle never said anything in anger to him at all. He also asked him, 'Isn't it true that you thought about killing both of them and realized that you had got nothing in the house to use as a weapon and for that reason you went to borrow the axe?' But Jackson told Linney that he had not borrowed the axe to kill Broddle and that he was in such a passion that he didn't know what he was doing. Linney pointed out that if he was in such a passion how was it that the neighbour didn't detect something was wrong? But Jackson had no answer to this question.

His defence, Mr Snowdon, then asked Mr Jackson how long he and his wife had been married and he replied, 'Fourteen years and we had never had a cross word until that night'. He stated to the jury that if Jackson had intended to kill Broddle that he could have done it. He had the axe in his hand and he was in a state of frenzy. He had found the letters when his wife went out at around 3.30pm and he had been thinking about her betrayal for six hours until she came home. Mr Snowdon said that up to this incident Mr Jackson had been a model father who loved his family. He had an excellent work record and did not drink very much at all. Any red-blooded man reading those letters would have sent him into a state of anger and it could be said that he was provoked beyond measure and that provocation in a murder case must decrease the charge to one of manslaughter.

The judge, Mr Justice Oliver, summed up for the jury, informing them that the letters showed the motive behind the attack and the prisoner had aroused some sympathy in the courtroom. He told them that one of the letters ended, 'I love you my true sweetheart', adding 'Peggy loves her daddy'. These words must have driven him to do something he was not normally capable of. The judge told the court that there was divorce proceedings pending and that the evidence showed that Jackson had never ever thought about being unfaithful to his wife and regretted the act as soon as it was done. He added:

> This is one of those cases where having heard all the evidence you have to decide whether you should reject the charge of attempted murder and also one of grievous bodily harm or you may find him not guilty of unlawful wounding. On the other hand you might feel that you can acquit him altogether. Everyone who has heard the case feels sympathy for the prisoner whose wife has carried on this sordid intrigue for years, but on the other hand an attack was made and cannot go unpunished.

The jury took very little time to bring in a not guilty verdict to attempted murder and that instead Jackson had been found guilty of unlawful wounding, but appealed to the judge for clemency. The judge appeared to be very pleased with the verdict and called Jackson to the dock where he sentenced him to four months' imprisonment, which, taking into account the time already spent in prison, meant his immediate release. It was reported that Superintendent W Kay of Rotherham police force had secured a place at Wombwell Main colliery for Jackson and it was established that he would live with his parents nearby. The judge looked down on the, by now smiling Jackson, and asked him, 'You will not let me down now will you?

'No sir' he replied 'I will not'.

The *Rotherham Advertiser*, in January 1942, reported that Jackson had requested the custody of the older child, Hilda (13). Once again he was represented by Mr J P Crehan, and his wife, still at the marital home, was represented by Mr F W Scorah of Sheffield. It seems that Mrs Jackson was still continuing her relationship with Broddle. Mr Crehan said, 'There was no application for the youngest child who it had been proven was not his.' He stated that if Hilda was given the option and wanted to stay with her mother he would still apply for custody, as his wife, whilst being in a relationship with another man who was not her husband, had proved herself not to be a fit mother. Mr Jackson told the magistrate that the eldest child was 'the only thing he had saved from his marriage'. Mr Scorah pronounced that in his opinion the child should remain with her mother until after the divorce had been heard. He pointed out that Mr Jackson had not complained about the way in which she had brought up the children in the past. The magistrate asked to see Hilda in his own chambers and the couple had to wait until he had spoken to her. He questioned her for about ten minutes and then asked Mr Scorah if the custody was to be discussed in the divorce court and when he replied that it was he stated that he would leave the matter to be decided at the divorce proceedings. It was later reported that the divorce was given to Mr Jackson, citing Broddle as the co-respondent.

Jackson was fortunate in this case to get such a sympathetic judge and they must have taken into account his formerly respectable and quiet nature. Any man finding out simultaneously that his wife was being unfaithful and his youngest child was not his must have been driven to distraction. Brooding on the matter for six hours led to the very extreme and violent attack on Broddle who was lucky to have survived.

CHAPTER 18

The Wicked Stepmother 1945

The body of Mrs Lilly White was found at 10.30am on Sunday, 11 February 1945, by a milk girl, Doreen Beach. No one could think of a motive for killing this quiet little woman, who was aged 54 and described as 'house-proud and respectable'. Doreen was employed by Thackeray's Farm at Brampton. Aged 15, she was a pupil at Maltby Grammar School. Doreen was so upset by the discovery of the body that she had to receive medical treatment. She regularly delivered milk to the house at Brampton Avenue, Thurcroft and did what she usually did on that fateful morning: calling out when she reached the back door. On receiving no reply, she pushed open the door to the scullery and saw the body of Mrs White lying on the floor, fully clothed. At the side of her was an upturned bicycle. Doreen ran to the nearest neighbours and they alerted the police.

When Superintendent L V Marshall of Rotherham West Riding police force arrived at the house, along with Chief Inspector Lee, they noted that the body had strangulation marks upon the neck. It looked from the position of them as if the murderer had been left handed. A house-to-house search was started to try and trace Lilly's activities on the Saturday, but it was reported that nothing had turned up. A reporter from the *Rotherham Advertiser* said that due to 'the mysterious circumstances surrounding the case' the CID from Rotherham and Wakefield were 'investigating jointly'.

On searching the house, Inspector Lee found almost no food in the pantry, but in a locked bedroom upstairs there were loaves of bread, margarine, pastries, chocolate, boiled sweets, eggs, jam, syrup, cake and bacon. There was nothing missing from the house and there appeared to be no motive for the crime. When the inspector spoke to the neighbours the life of

Brampton Bierlow where the girl who found the body, Doreen Beech, was employed to deliver milk. Rotherham Local Studies & Archives

this woman was revealed. She was described as being quiet and reserved and had little to do with the neighbours; but was polite to them when spoken to. She was the second wife of Mr Richard Bushfield White and they had married in 1939. The couple had no children of their own, but she was stepmother to the large family of his first wife. The inspector, when he checked out the background of Lilly White, found that she had spent most of her life at Pitsmoor, near Sheffield, where some of her family still lived. On the death of her father in 1908 she trained as a nurse, leaving the town when she was 24 to work in a mental hospital in Kesteven. She qualified as a night sister but had a nervous breakdown in 1930 and returned back to Sheffield where she met Mr White in 1938.

Mr White's first wife had died in 1938, leaving seven children: four sons and three daughters; and three of the sons still lived at home. They were Eric (24), Thomas (18) and Clifford (12). It was reported that another son (20) was serving overseas with the forces and all the daughters lived elsewhere. The neighbours reported that she was very fond of her stepchildren and in particular Clifford. It appeared that both Eric and Thomas were deaf, but they both were in full-time employment, managing their disability quite well. Mr White, who was

Thurcroft Colliery, where Eric White and his brother were employed. Rotherham Local Studies & Archives

also deaf, was working as a joiner in London and had done since September 1944, repairing some of the bomb-shattered buildings in the capital. Consequently, he only came home occasionally. The neighbours told the inspector that the house was always clean and tidy and no one could give a reason why this well-liked woman had been killed.

The children of Mr White were questioned and they stated that she had been alive at 10.30am, the last time she had been seen. It was noted that Eric had some scratches on his hands and face, but said that they had happened at work. When asked if he knew anyone who bore any malice sufficient to do his stepmother any injury, he stated that he didn't. Detective Sergeant Stubbs noted that all three of her stepsons took the news of her death very 'unconcernedly'.

The police were baffled and a post mortem was undertaken by Dr P Lindsey Sutherland, the county pathologist, on Monday 12 February. This revealed a dark secret which was not announced to the press. There was much speculation about the finding of the body reported in the press and an inquest was held on 13 February at the Thurcroft Colliery Institute, where the coroner, Dr P Lockwood, told the jury that he had not had a copy of the post mortem findings and so the inquest would merely serve for the purpose of identification; and then would be adjourned until more enquiries had been made. The identification was made by Mr White and the adjourned inquest date was fixed for 23 February.

The funeral took place in the afternoon of Saturday 17 February. By the time of the adjourned inquest was held it was announced that one of the stepsons, Eric, had been charged with the murder and that he would appear in front of the magistrate on 24 February where he was remanded until 9 March. This was as a result of the post mortem which revealed that Lilly had died at approximately 5.00am on Saturday and was not alive at 10.30am on Sunday 11 February. As a result of this the police went to the house to talk to Eric on Friday 16 February. He admitted that he had killed her and that he wanted to change his statement. Because of Eric's deafness, the police were very careful to ensure that he understood what was being said to him and that a verbal and written charge of murder was made against him. Eric asked if he could write out his own statement, which he did, taking just over two hours to complete. Because of this, which was corroborated by the other stepchildren at the hearing, a very different story came out about the horrors that Mrs Lilly White had inflicted on her stepfamily. Eric was arrested and when charged said, 'I have said all I can' and he was brought to Rotherham police station that same evening by Detective Sergeant Stubbs. At the magistrates' court, on 17 February, the prisoner was remanded again to the following Monday as there was still no post-mortem results available. For this hearing he had been provided with headphones and a loud speaker.

Finally, Eric was brought into the magistrates' court on Friday 23 March 1945 and his statement was read out by the prosecution, Mr A A Gordon Clarke. In his statement, Eric wrote that he had not liked his stepmother on sight and did not want to attend the wedding because of this, but was persuaded to do so by his father. He said that when she first moved in she was alright for a few days but one day he came downstairs when she was washing the floor and she started 'rowing with him and told him to get out'. She was the same with his brother and sisters who could not stand her.

Lilly was not the quiet, respectable person as seen by the neighbours but a quarrelsome woman who starved all the family systematically. Eric wrote about only having two slices of bread and dripping for breakfast and tea during the week, but they were allowed butter on a Sunday as well as a small piece of cake. His stepmother, however, 'had butter every day of the week and she had more to eat than us'. He stated that his meals were almost the same every day and Lilly always made a lot of vegetables in order to eke out any of the cheap cuts of meat; and these vegetables were re-heated at every mid time meal, some times up to four days later. Despite this, both himself and Thomas had to pay her 'board' money which they had to give her every week. If they complained, she would throw the food at them and call them 'greedy pigs'. She alone had access to the bedroom and would stuff herself with cake and chocolate to which the family were not allowed to enter.

Eric described the bed which he was forced to share with his two brothers and said that the pillows were so dirty that he asked her to change them, which she refused to do. He said the same pillows had been on the bed since she moved into the house. The blankets were washed only once every two or three weeks and they were inadequate. He had asked for more but she told him that she had none and they were forced to use coats on the bed when it was really cold. They had never had new blankets and the mattress had stuffing coming out of it. The bedroom in which all the male members of the family slept was cluttered with rubbish, such as a bedstead and a table and he told his stepmother that the bedroom was not big enough for three men to share. She was also very abusive to him. All the family were frightened to upset her and she would row with them on a regular basis. Even his sister, Dorothy, who was now married, had been left without food and remembered crying with hunger. He wrote that as a teenager he had suffered from tuberculosis and, as a consequence, had to go away from home three times a year where he would be looked after really well and the food was good. He wrote that 'those were the happiest days of my life and I was miserable when I had to return home'.

Eric worked in the coal mines and he said that if he was on the morning shift, he only had some tea and two slices of bread, but that he would not complain because she would 'start rowing which I don't like'. On the afternoon shift he came home to a drink of cocoa, which she knew he hated, and two slices of bread. Sometimes he would be so hungry that he would buy something from the colliery canteen as he knew there would be little food for him when he got home. Lilly also made him wash his own work clothes which were very dirty after a shift in the mines, saying that she refused to touch 'those dirty things'. There had been many times when he had nothing to eat before going to work. He had told his father about it once when he came home and his father and stepmother had rowed about it and he admitted that because of his deafness he hadn't heard the entire row, but he had heard his father tell her to get out. He said that he wanted to go into lodgings, but was unable to leave his little brother. Quite often Clifford was crying because he was so hungry and Eric would give him some of his food. When Clifford refused to eat his dinner or his tea because he didn't like it Lilly would take it away from him and he often had to go to school hungry; and they had to do without sugar in their tea because she said there was none; but Eric knew that there was plenty in the bedroom. She refused to wash Clifford's clothes or buy him new ones and Eric stated that he was ashamed to see the condition of his brother's clothes. It must have made some impression on her, as when he received the letter from his father stating he was coming home for the weekend, she told Eric to get Clifford a coat from the second-hand stall in the market, but he couldn't find one and she was forced to buy him a new suit and some boots.

His father came home on Friday 2 February and went back to London on the following Tuesday. But he stated that she was no easier to live with when his father had been home and the couple were continually arguing, usually about the way she treated the family; and they all learned to not upset her if they could help it. But on the night of the murder Eric had, once again, asked her to make some more room in the bedroom as it was getting cramped for the three of them to share a bed, when there was another bedroom not being used. She refused, calling him 'a lousy swine and a bastard' and he became very upset 'thinking and thinking that this wouldn't be happening if my mother was still alive'. He went to bed and lay there with his brothers, who were asleep at the side of him and described how he was getting more and more upset. He went downstairs and told her that he was sleeping in the chair in the scullery that night and she started to swear at him and use 'bad language'. She raised a hand to him and he slapped it away and 'she tried to scratch my face and hands and I pushed her away and she fell against the mangle'. He walked away from her and told her that he was going for a walk and went towards the back door to open it. Suddenly, he felt her hands grab his shoulders and he grabbed her round the neck and the couple fell over and he landed on top of her. He told the police that he couldn't remember much more about that night, but he did remember straightening the cloth on the sofa and turning the lights out before he went to bed.

The prosecutor, Mr A A Gordon Clarke, told the jury that Eric's statement revealed that his relations with his stepmother had been anything but harmonious and that she had been miserly in the food given to the stepchildren, yet in another room there was a large quantity of food which had been hidden away. Also in the room were four drawers containing pillow cases, bedding and blankets. He told the magistrate that the police had found the body lying on the floor of the scullery, along with several upturned items: a watering can, false teeth and a pair of spectacles which indicated that a struggle had taken place. The injury had been made by someone left-handed and matched that of Eric whose hands and face was scratched. His first statement was that he had left his stepmother on the Sunday morning unharmed at 10.30am. When he was visited by the police the following Friday he was asked if he had told the truth and he admitted that he had lied, saying, 'I did go downstairs and what has happened has been worrying me all week.' Inspector Marshall was sent for and Eric was cautioned. Dr Sutherland testified that death was due to asphyxia from strangling and the bruising on the body of the deceased woman was consistent with a struggle.

It was reported that the prisoner had taken no interest in the proceedings, which was understandable if he was deaf. Anyone with any understanding of working with deaf people are aware that even with our modern-day hearing aids, it is sometimes necessary to stand in a good light in front of the person and attempt clear speech. Obviously in a busy magistrates' court this was impossible as most of the remarks are addressed towards the magistrate and the jury. Mr Clarke, for the defence, stated that he hoped to have some kind of hearing appliance for the assizes for the testimony of Thomas White, but that he did not intend to call him or the prisoner to the stand for the time being. It was reported that he would have better equipment for his deafness at the assizes, which confirmed the police belief that he was guilty and gave him little chance to defend himself against any other witness statement. However, the other brother, Clifford, arrived and he told the court that Eric was a kind and thoughtful brother, who had given him some of his food when he knew that Clifford was hungry. Their father stated that his wife was 'aggressive to his sons and she used bad language, but they had never answered her back as far as he was aware'. The jury, after hearing these statements, had no option but to send Eric for trial at the Leeds Assizes for the murder of his stepmother.

Eric was brought into the court at Leeds on 23 April 1945. Thankfully, by now he was equipped with a set of headphones which amplified the voices of witnesses. His father and his brother had headphones too.

PC Pepper stated that when he went to the house he found that two of the three bedrooms were unoccupied. The one bedroom which was shared by all three sons was in a dirty condition and had no sheets. There was only one pillow which had no cover on and the blankets were filthy. When Clifford White took the stand he told the court that he wanted more food. He also told them that he did not want to sleep alone because he was frightened and so had slept in the bed with his older brothers. His brother, Thomas Frederick White, said that his stepmother was always nagging and calling him 'bad names'. When he asked her for more food she told him that if he wanted more food he would have to pay her more lodge money. The deceased woman's husband, Richard White, stated that 'if fault had to be proved that it was on her side'. He said to the judge, 'She told my sons to get out, but I told her if they go I will too', and she calmed down.

Mr G H Streatfield, for the defence, in his summing up said to the jury:

> You have heard things which must have shocked you and you probably had no idea that such things went on in this country. It is a lamentable story of a family, happy enough when their mother was alive. Then there came into this family a hard stepmother. This woman was powerfully-built, overbearing, nagging and thrifty, a hoarder and a miser. Eric White's statement says he did not go downstairs with the intention of killing her and in fact he tried to get away from her. If you take the view that the prisoner was acting in self defence then I ask for a verdict of acquittal or failing that a verdict of manslaughter.

The jury agreed and in only an hour came back into the court with a verdict of not guilty of murder but guilty of manslaughter. Mr Justice Humphrey agreed and sentenced him to twelve months in prison, excusing the light sentence as being 'an exceptional case which might be met by an exceptionally lenient sentence'. The prisoner thanked the judge, stating that he did not want to kill his stepmother and was sorry for all the trouble he had caused to all concerned.

This tragic case, thankfully, was dealt with as sensitively as was possible. Any man, or woman, suffering such provocation over a length of time might be in a similar position as Eric White found himself. It might be added that the young man's father surely could have done something to prevent it happening, but chose to ignore that which he didn't see.

CHAPTER 19

A Sexual Pervert 1950

This next case is not so unfamiliar to our modern ears, but the way in which it was reported and the comments made in court at the time are truly shocking. The political correctness of our time was unknown back in the 1950s, but at the risk of offending people I have recorded many of the comments as they were printed in the newspapers of the period, in an attempt to give an insight into the intolerant and prejudiced way in which the victim was seen.

When the body of a man was found on a footpath on the East Herringthorpe estate it was a great shock to the person who found the deceased, not so much because he was dead, rather than because he was dressed in women's clothing.

Frank James, a bus inspector, was going to work at 4.00am on 1 July 1950 when he saw what he thought was a woman lying on the pavement. As he got closer he could see that a wig had fallen off and it was in fact a man. The man's face was bruised and bloody and he was lying face down. James went to the telephone kiosk in Laudsdale Road and rang the police. Inspector Whitely arrived and met the man at the kiosk and they both went to see the body a short distance away. The body was lying face down in a pool of blood. Such was the ferocity of the attack that there were splashes of blood up to 11 feet 9 inches away. The man's dentures were broken into three pieces and had fallen near to his head. He was wearing a green and white dress and a brown swagger coat, a green felt beret and a man's sport shorts, green woollen gloves, brown silk stockings, a neck scarf, white high-heeled canvas shoes and a dark handbag with a zipper. He had no identification on him. The police issued a description and asked for anyone who could recognize him or the clothing to come forward. The body was taken to the mortuary at Dalton. When Inspector Whitely helped the pathologist to undress the body they found a brassier stuffed with socks.

Patrick John Cooney, who savagely beat his victim to death. Rotherham Local Studies & Archives

At 2.00pm a young man entered the police station at Dalton and gave himself up as the killer of the unknown man. He made a statement telling the police the events of the previous evening. The man's name was Patrick Cooney. Eighteen months earlier he had come from Scotland to Rotherham to work in the mines. He was aged 25 and the previous night had gone out to the Dalton Top Club where he met a friend, Reg Kelsall. They had a few drinks and played a few games of snooker. On leaving the pub at about 11.00pm he, Reg and Jim Wood, the brother of his girlfriend, went to Wood's house and had some supper. Patrick then left alone to go home to his lodgings in Arundel Avenue. He had almost reached home when he saw a woman standing on her own and shouted, 'Goodnight love.' She replied, 'Just a minute.' He went back to her and she told him that she had arranged to meet someone called Jim who had stood her up, so he agreed to see her home. He put his arm through hers and they walked towards Dalton Brook. When they got to a circle of grass he asked her to sit down with him for a while, but she pulled away saying, 'Come on, come on.' Cooney put his arms around her and kissed her and she didn't resist. He pulled her closer to him and he told the police, 'I felt something was wrong'; and at that point he knew that 'she' was in fact a man. Cooney continued with his statement, telling the police that he turned to walk away from her and felt her pulling at his shoulders, saying 'Don't go, it will be alright.' He described being so angry and disgusted with himself that he lost control and punched the man in the face several times in order to 'teach him a lesson'. The man fell to the floor, his wig fell off and Cooney saw a bald patch at the top of his head. He then sat astride him, punching and punching at his face and body. He had admitted being angry and disgusted that he had fallen for the idea that this was a man and not a woman.

The man didn't speak during the attack and Cooney, still furious, turned him over and smashed his face against the pavement as he did so. Then Cooney got up and ran all the way back to his lodgings where he went upstairs to bed. He shared a room with a man called Thomas Lynch who was awake when Cooney got home. He told Lynch what had happened, stating that he had met a woman who had whistled after him and he had taken her for a walk. When he put his arms around her he realized that 'she' was a man and admitted to Lynch that 'he had punched him once or twice'.

The following morning both Cooney and Lynch were up and out for work at 5.45am to start their shift at the pit. When Cooney's shift had finished he came up to the surface to find other miners laughing at the fact that a body had been found at Dalton Brook dressed in women's clothing and he knew immediately that it was the man he had attacked the previous night. He waited for Lynch to come up to the surface and told him what had happened and that he was going to have to given himself up. He asked Lynch to go with him to the Dalton police station. Without going back to his lodgings, he went straight to the station at 2.10pm and said, 'It's me you want, I did it', bursting into tears. Cooney was charged with the murder of 'an unknown man'.

Whilst enquiries were still being made into the identity of the deceased man, who was aged about 37 years of age, a post mortem was held by Dr E Price of Leeds, consultant pathologist. He noted that the face was entirely covered in blood, but underneath he saw rouge, face powder and lipstick. The man had two black eyes, a broken nose, fracture's of the upper and lower jaws, lacerations in the left corner of the mouth and on his neck was bruising consistent with the use of finger tips. There was haemorrhaging beneath the structure of the voice box and gullet. The heart and lungs showed signs of asphyxia and there were many abrasions on the wrist. He told the court later that he also found evidence that the man was 'a sexual pervert'. This was not explained in the newspaper of the period as it was too delicate, but what it probably means was that he had recognized the evidence of anal penetration.

Meanwhile, the wife of the dead man had identified the body. She told the police that it was her husband, Kenneth Charles Crowe, a woodwork teacher at Rotherham Grammar School. They had two daughters, aged 11 and 13. Mrs Crowe could not explain how he came to be wearing her clothes. She had never known him to wear her clothes before or even to go out at night. His body had been found just a short distance from Hounsfield Road where they lived.

Kenneth Charles Crowe. Rotherham Local Studies & Archives

It appears that the night of 31 July/1 August Crowe had seen his wife and two girls leave the house about 8.00pm and he was later seen in the garden by a neighbour, watering some flowers. He appeared to be quite normal and chatted animatedly to the neighbour, saying that he was going to have a 'quiet night in'. Later that evening a 'woman' was seen walking up and down the street at the junction of Norwood Street and Doncaster Road, Dalton. A witness, Frederick Snowdon, was talking to some friends on Dalton Road between 10.45pm and 11.30pm and noticed the woman walking up and down as 'she' passed him several times. He didn't think it was anything unusual, just a girl waiting for someone she had planned to meet.

Cooney was brought into the West Riding Police Court on Wednesday 3 August. He was dressed smartly in a fawn jacket and brown trousers. He appeared to be slightly nervous but composed. The prosecutor, Mr E C Jones, started the proceedings by saying, 'It is obvious from the evidence that this man was a sexual pervert.'

Mrs Crowe appeared as the first witness, stating that she had identified the man as being her husband. The clothes that the deceased had been wearing were shown to her and she

The proximity showing how near the body of the deceased was found to his home.
Rotherham Local Studies & Archives

identified them as being her own, apart from the gloves which had belonged to her daughter. She told the court that on the evening of 31 July she had gone to Dinnington for the night and taken her daughters with her. She had made arrangements to see her husband the following day. Mrs Crowe had reported her husband as missing when he had not arrived at the appointed time. When shown the body she recognized him, but was very shocked at seeing him in her own clothes. The handbag was also hers and when she was shown it, she saw that inside there was a piece of rope which appeared to be her daughter's skipping rope. Mrs Crowe told the police that she had never seen the wig before. She was also shown drawings of herself and her husband tied to a chair. These had been drawn by her husband and had been in his possession the night he had died.

Friends of Cooney appeared and gave testaments to the man's character. He was known to be a good worker, 'one of the best' according to Reg Kelsall, who had known him for a long time. He told the court that Cooney had made a lot of friends at the pit where he worked. His other friend, Lynch, told the court that Cooney had no idea that he had killed the man dressed as a woman and when he heard that a dead body had been found dressed in woman's clothing 'went white'.

Evidence was heard from other witnesses, but the jury had no option but to send Cooney for trial at the assizes where he appeared on 25 November 1950 in front of the judge, Mr

Finnemore. Richard Green appeared for the defence and Mr H R B Shepherd for the prosecution. Cooney's aunt, who had come from Ayr for the trial, told the judge that she was his only living relative as Cooney had lost both parents while he was young and had been brought up by his grandmother in Scotland.

Testimony revealed that Cooney had some experience in the boxing ring and was very strong. When Cooney gave his evidence he described blow for blow the attack on Crowe. The only part he could not remember distinctly was putting his hands around Crowe's throat.

Dr Price listed the man's injuries and stated that after beating him Cooney had turned the body over and smashed the deceased face into the ground. The reason Cooney gave for this was that he 'wanted to teach him a lesson and to make sure that he would not go out dressed like that again'. Dr Price revealed that the cause of death was strangulation accelerated by shock caused by the fracture of the upper and lower jaw. He stated once more that evidence from the post mortem showed that Crowe was a 'sexual pervert and that he was in fact an habitual addict to a certain form of perversion'.

Mr Green pointed out to the jury that everyone who knew Cooney had given him a good character and he had never had a history of violence before. He stated that he had been provoked by his discovery and had been unable to control himself in an attack that was very out of character. He had not had any intention to murder anyone and intention had to be present for the crime to be one of murder. He then said, 'It could be said that by dressing up in women's clothes it could be sufficient grounds for reducing the charge from murder to manslaughter.' Green asked the court, 'Is he to be blamed for hitting out? A man may surely defend himself from the importuning of a homosexual.'

Mr Shepherd asked Cooney if Crowe had been violent towards him or had tried to defend himself from the attack. Cooney admitted that he hadn't. He pointed out to the jury that Cooney had walked away from the man, knowing that at the very least he was quite severely injured. Even if he didn't intend to murder him the intention was to inflict grievous bodily harm.

Furthermore, when Crowe fell onto his back, he was in no position to defend himself from a fit young man.

The judge told the jury that they had to decide whether this was a case of murder or manslaughter. He said, 'You should not be put off by disgust at the behaviour of Crowe unless you thought it was relevant to the case.'

The jury retired for two hours and when they returned the foreman told the court that they had found the prisoner guilty of manslaughter. The judge sentenced Cooney to five years, saying to him:

> You did not intend to murder Crowe and it might be proper to say that the attack was justified. You are a man of good character and are well thought of by your peers. Crowe was a man of education who in the course of his profession was put in charge of boys. What it was that creature was up to on the night of 31st July may never be realized. What tricks was he seeking to play on some innocent passer by? It is a thousand pities that the accused man had the dreadful misfortune to be accosted by the deceased.

This damning summing up emphasizes the disgust felt at the time for people who did not fit into the sexual behaviour which should be expected by society. The judge in his speech almost apologizes for sending Cooney to prison for this vicious attack. Indeed, the blood spatter being so far away indicated the ferocity of this one-sided assault. Homophobia is prevalent throughout this case as is indicated by the comments made from professional people. What we have to bear in mind is that men could be imprisoned for having relations with another man during this period and to be a transvestite was not understood at all. Homosexuality only became decriminalized in Britain in 1967. Certainly there was no doubt that Cooney was well thought of by his friends. After his sentence the court were told that his friends had paid for his defence, even though he would have been entitled to legal aid. At the time of his sentence £200 had been collected for him from concerts and subscriptions made for him led by Jim Wood; and it was reported that his friends had also gone to the assizes in a bus to support their former work colleague. Nevertheless, in our much more enlightened world, the battering which led to murder was a vicious crime on a man unable to defend from a fit and stronger younger man.

* * *

The murders in this book are a product of the pressures of life of living through the war years as well as other times of instability when the taking of a life, whether others or your own seems to be the only solution. Many of these cases indicate that state of mind impinged on the decision-making, whilst others are cold blooded and calculated acts. What drives a person to commit murder is not fully answered in this book and is a topic which is not always known even today. But the people within its pages and the crimes that were committed were real. However, it has to be said that Rotherham is a good place to live and has much other history to offer to those who are interested. Crime and murder is only a small part of the story. I hope that you have enjoyed this trip into Rotherham in the first fifty years of the twentieth century as much as I have.

Index